ITALY'S OTHER ISLAND

Mirto Sappé remembers his first car; £38 in October 1957.

'In fact the car lost its gear box as I was returning to the Moorings, having collected my first driving licence from St Martin Public Hall.

We could go to St Helier and back to Gorey on one gear, but had to use the coast road.

My second Austin was exactly the same, but in much better condition. It cost only £8 and had green leather seats.

The old lady (previous) owner had hit a tree, so we took the front axle from the first one and then the second one went very well until I met June the following spring and had to get a more modern, fashionable car... which was a split windscreen, two tone Morris Minor!!!'

ITALY'S OTHER ISLAND

The Italian Community and the Making of Modern Jersey

By Hamish Marett-Crosby

Louis Roederer Regional Wine Writer of the Year 2007

Le Prix de Champagne Lanson 2003 & 2004

CROSBY MEDIA & PUBLISHING LTD

Published in 2017 by
Crosby Media and Publishing Ltd
La Cohue
St John
Jersey
JE3 4FN

Printed by
Dolman Scott
1 High Street,
Thatcham,
Berks,
RG19 3JG.

CONTENTS

Renzo Martin on Gorey Pier
Photograph by courtesy of the Jersey Evening Post

FOREWORD

By Cavaliere RENZO MARTIN, Honorary Consular Agent for Italy in the Channel Islands 1978 - 2016

IT was a long time ago that I came to Jersey as a young man anxious to make my way in the world within my chosen profession. In fact it was so long ago that I might be excused for not being too exact about the date. Suffice it to say that I was one of the early groups of Italians, my fellow countrymen, who came to Jersey to work in the hospitality industry. The numbers quickly swelled and by the mid-1960s there were over 3,000 of us here. Many went back home but those who stayed, in all manner of roles within the hotel and catering Industry, helped to form the basis of a new and vibrant tourism sector in Jersey.

But now the world has changed. Hotels cater for a different market and the full-board tourist has long gone; indeed, not that many visitors book evening meals in advance. Similarly, fashions in the dining rooms have also changed beyond all recognition: the lamps have gone, gueridon service is no more and the brigades of old have been consigned to the history books. That is unfortunate for it was the hierarchical nature of the brigade that created a breeding ground of professionalism and the opportunity for even the most humble commis to aspire to the rank of maître d'hôtel. He was arguably one of the key people in the catering industry; the man around whom the whole operation of the restaurant or hotel dining room revolved.

However times change and the styles of presentation and service for which many of my colleagues of the time honed their professional skills are no more. That is not to say they were better or worse than what is on offer now, only different. The great brigades moving from hotel to hotel are no more and who, these days, has heard of gueridon service?

But although the dining room staff members were perhaps the most visible members of the Italian community in Jersey, one should not forget the others who worked as chefs, receptionists, barmen, buyers and eventually hotel managers who all played their part in the creation of what many say remains the Italian legacy to Jersey. Together they created the foundations of what were the golden years of tourism in Jersey and from which emerged the modern Jersey tourism offering.

It had long been a matter of concern to me that the memories of the time in which Italians provided so much for the early development of Jersey's tourism industry were being forgotten. That would, I used to think, be a tragedy. I firmly believe our contribution to that industry, which Tourism Committees of the times would highlight to advertise the Island, is something that should be not only remembered but also acknowledged and applauded.

I was thrilled, therefore, to hear from an old friend, Hamish Marett-Crosby - a well known broadcaster, journalist and former wine merchant - that he was planning to take up this challenge and so do his bit to save those memories before, with the passing of years, they are all lost.

Talking to Hamish, I was particularly pleased to hear that he views one of the great achievements of the Italian community to be one of successful integration. I have long been of the opinion that we have blended into the community without losing sight of our origins. Those of us who have done well personally are viewed, in Hamish's words, not as successful Italian businessman, but as successful businessmen who happen to be Italian. I agree wholeheartedly with him as to the importance of that distinction.

Hamish has been a friend to the Italian Community in Jersey for many years and his work in researching and writing this book will be invaluable in preserving our own heritage, thus reminding the world of our legacy to this Island. Maybe we can hope that his work will encourage others to examine different aspects of this little piece of Jersey-Italian history.

I wish him every success and hope that many people will read this book and so help preserve the memories of our achievement, the Italian contribution to the history of Jersey tourism.

Renzo Martin
Jersey 2017

ACKNOWLEDGMENTS

It goes without saying, or at least it should do, that without the willing help of every member of the Italian community to whom I have talked while researching this project, there would have been no book. Jersey's debt to what they have achieved is the subject of this book, my debt to them is immense, and I am deeply grateful for all their help and encouragement.

I also gratefully acknowledge the helpfulness of BBC Jersey for giving me use of the interview recordings originally made for the programme, *The Italians in Jersey.*

Tino Rossi of La Capannina should be thanked, or blamed, as he first gave me the idea of writing a book rather than talking round the subject.

There are others deserving of thanks and recognition, in particular Alasdair Crosby of Crosby Media and Publishing who devoted so much (he might feel too much) of his time in helping me through the complicated process of getting this book published.

The Jersey Evening Post was generous in allowing me to use some of their photographs for which I thank them. In that same area I must thank all the many Italians who sent me their own pictorial memories of their time here, thank you for trusting me with them and I am sorry I could not use them all.

Italo Miorin, the former *Fiduciario* of AMIRA Jersey, made his private archive available to me, which I found a treasure trove of memory. And so my thanks to him, not only for his help but also his encouragement.

To the members of the Italian community who suffered my endless questions with good grace, I have already thanked them for helping me with details of their story but I must also thank them for their patience and forbearing. It has been a wonderful time of discovery that has unlocked many memories for me and I hope it will be the same for all those who read this book.

I have had immense encouragement from the former consular agent of Italy in the Channel Islands, Renzo Martin, and I doubt if the book would have been finished as soon as has been the case, without the presence at the end of the phone of his successor, Serafina Jones - Venticinque.

To my Wife, Jeannine, who encouraged me to take up this project, I can only say thank-you, for I really do not think you knew what you were letting yourself in for. You spent many hours checking the text and suggesting different ways of presenting the information.

Finally there has to be a special mention of the Berni Trust, established by the late Frank Berni of Berni Inns. The Trust is a great public benefactor in Jersey and is also very keen to support the Italian community in Jersey as well as to highlight, and so preserve, the Italian heritage. The support of the Trustees in this project has been extraordinarily generous and is now publically and very gratefully acknowledged.

Hamish Marett-Crosby
Jersey 2017

INTRODUCTION

By the author, Hamish Marett-Crosby

'BUT do you think there are people interested in us waiters?'

It was a straight question asked of me by a retired local restaurateur, Franco Gatti, who many will remember as the flamboyant proprietor of the Restaurant de la Poste. By the end of this book you will be able to answer that question.

Some time ago, when working at BBC Radio Jersey, I produced a 60-minute radio documentary called 'The Italians in Jersey'. It was based on interviews with some of the better known Italian restaurateurs and maîtres and was made in an attempt to throw some light on the long association the Island had with those Italians who now call Jersey their home.

What surprised me during and after the making of this radio programme was that so many people had no idea about the size and importance of the contribution by the Jersey Italians to the development of tourism in this Island. Despite what they accomplished, the Italians are in danger of being forgotten about. The extraordinary influence they achieved has been over-written in the popular memory bank by future waves of immigration. Very few of my Jersey or British friends had any appreciation of the revolution they helped bring about in Jersey's tourism offering, a revolution far in excess of the pizza/pasta restaurants that remain as a dim reminder of what once was.

I suppose I was looking at their reaction from a privileged position, for I had worked with many Italians during my time as a wine merchant, had got to know them well and was proud to call many of them friends. I had an Italian business partner, Eric Ruaro, and together we imported perhaps the largest range of Italian wines that the Island had ever seen. I became involved in an Italian professional organisation, AMIRA, and travelled with them promoting Jersey. I felt sad, therefore, that their immense contribution could be forgotten within a generation.

One day I found some of the original interviews for that programme and I gave a copy of one original conversation to the interviewee's widow. 'Thank you,' she said. 'Now the grandchildren will get to know their grandfather.'

At around the same time Tino Rossi of La Capannina told me that many of his customers loved talking about the old days and they had enjoyed the radio programme, so I really should be preserving these memories in written form. 'What are you waiting for?' he asked.

It was then that the desire to write this book crystallised. I interviewed many more members of the Italian community - not everyone by a long chalk - but enough to create a picture of the times. Enough also to allow the descendents of all Jersey Italians the opportunity to get to know the world in which their fathers and grandfathers had succeeded, thereby giving them, the next generation, a better start in life than they could ever have had back in the Italy they left behind.

That is the genesis of this book. It is not, nor was it ever meant to be, a detailed story of all the Italians who made Jersey their home, that is a study waiting for a qualified social historian. Nor is it a history of every Italian-owned or Italian-managed restaurant that this Island has known.

It is a personal snapshot of a time when a relatively small group of barmen, waiters, maîtres and chefs arrived in Jersey bringing with them a level of professionalism, knowledge, experience and skills that the Island had not seen before.

As a group, they were highly visible, punched well above their weight and their legacy is enormous; indeed those in the industry with long memories believe that without their contribution, the Island's catering industry would not be as it is today. The Italians opened up Jersey to European catering influences, and their success was a major feature in Jersey tourism advertising.

I am well aware that the Italian contribution to Jersey's tourism industry was by no means limited to the dining room. The numbers of successful chefs, other members of the kitchen brigades, barmen, hotel managers, guest-house proprietors, front-of-house professionals and others within the hotel trade were sufficient to make an onlooker feel that Jersey really had become 'Italy's Other Island.'

However, this book is a personal recollection of those times and what was, to many Jersey residents, as well as visitors, the most visible aspect of the Italian presence in the dining rooms. It is also a personal recollection of my interaction with the Italians whom I had the pleasure of knowing.

Furthermore, the cultural zeitgeist of the time was to view the maître - in the hotel dining room or as the owner manager of the restaurant - as the lynch-pin of the operation. That has changed now and the chef has become the flag bearer. Nevertheless, the Italian contribution to the kitchens and to hotel management should not be understated.

This book is not only a snapshot of the catering industry managed and run by the Italians from the 1950s onwards but it is, above all, a very individual snapshot at that. It is based on talking to some of those who worked through those times and it is my view, an outsider's view, of the community. As I implied, I have neither the time nor the space to include every 'Jersey-Italian' in this look back in time. To all the Italians in Jersey, especially those I know but have not had the time to approach for their own memories, I can only say that I am aware, and after reading this book, everyone else should be aware of the contribution to their legacy made by each and every one of you.

Those who came to Jersey as young men in the 1950s, 1960s, even into the start of the 1970s, are now well into retirement age, so perhaps this is the last opportunity for us not only to take a look back at a very special time in Jersey's tourism development, but also to thank them for their contribution. There are bound to be omissions. Many might feel that other stories of the time should have been included but, as I said, this is a personal remembrance, a snapshot, a simple selection but also one developed out of respect, gratitude and combined with much affection.

If I have somehow managed to get elements of the story wrong or missed out something important, I can only apologise. The fault lies with the storyteller, not those who gave him the information.

'But do you think there are people interested in us waiters?'

I leave it for you to judge best how to answer that question.

Hamish Marett-Crosby
Jersey 2017

The waiters race was a feature of the tourist calendar in the 1950s and through the 1960s. It always attracted large crowds as can be seen. This comes from the early 1950s. (Photograph by Courtesy of the Jersey Evening Post).

Chapter 1

ARRIVING

THEY came, they saw - and in a sense - they conquered.

The story of the Italians leaving their own country in search of work and (with luck and a following wind) creating a niche for themselves wherever they arrived is a common one.

It was not just in Jersey. In the United Kingdom this immigration saw a major 'colony' of Italians in London and the creation of Little Italy in Clerkenwell, followed by a move - by some - into catering or catering supplies. In other parts of the country, Italian ice cream became a much sought-after treat that over the generations became an indulgence for the masses. But, whatever else they did, catering seemed to be a natural fit.

An article in The Independent four decades ago considered the way Italian cooking in the United Kingdom had taken on its own character and so became, on occasions, noticeably different from the source of its inspiration back in Italy. The paper went on to refer to a previously published overview of restaurants in London to make its point.

The quoted article described a scene in a restaurant where the head waiter greeting you and guiding you to your table would be looking forward to retiring to his villa he had commissioned to be built in the hills overlooking the Po Valley in Northern Italy. His assistant, presenting you with the menu, already had his villa somewhere in the foothills above the valley of the Po under the first stages of construction. Meanwhile the junior who served the food believed that concealed somewhere under the plates being placed in front of the diners, were the plans for his own dream villa, which would rise out of the ground back near his family village overlooking the River Po.

In other words, there had already been several generations of Italians working in London restaurants and hotel dining rooms at the time of that published overview of London's Italian restaurants (which, by the way, had been written in the 1870s); the London-based Italians had already staked their claim to the catering trade.

This, of course, should come as no surprise to the eight or nine million people who every week for two months in 2016, while watching the Independent Television series, Victoria, were kept up to date with the life of the palace chef, Francatelli. Charles Francatelli was a real person; he was no invention to give colour to a plot of a drama hampered by the fact that we all knew, before the series had even begun, what was going to happen.

He was an Anglo-Italian and one of the culinary celebrities of this time. He had his natural skills honed by studying under the colossus of international cooking Antonin Carême, one of the greatest chefs of history who was among the founders (some would say the founder) of French haute cuisine.

Famous for adapting the best of Italian and French cuisine, Francatelli was regarded as a leading chef in Victorian London and spent most of his career in Britain directing the kitchens of several aristocrats and nobleman, including for a short time being appointed maître d'hôtel and 'Chief Cook in Ordinary' to the Queen. He also managed to write four best-selling books of recipes and cooking hints.

In an off-the-cuff remark, often quoted, he once speculated that he could feed a thousand families every day on the food that was wasted in London. Quite how he would have reacted to the waste built into the food chain and food preparation, both commercially and at home today, one hesitates to think, but to make his point he produced 'A Plain Cookery Book for the Working Classes', which contained information of practical value to those who struggled to make ends meet. This included economical treats such as cow-heel broth, bubble and squeak and sheep's pluck (parts of a sheep traditionally found in haggis).

In 1861 came 'The Cook's Guide and Housekeeper's & Butler's Assistant', which became a standard book of reference for any well-managed household, containing over a thousand recipes as well as special diets for the sick and feeble.

Of course, London was not the only place where the Italians came and flourished. But the essential fact to bear in mind was that by the 1950s, they had been a force in the catering trade in England for 150 years at least. In Jersey, however, probably because of its Island status and so - to a degree - being off the map, that particular social evolution had not been imported.

Immigrants to Jersey seeking work (largely from France) had tended to come for the season to work on the farms but, with the growing importance of the tourist industry, the very efficient radar of Italians seeking work abroad homed in on Jersey and by the 1930s a trickle of them had come to work in the Jersey hotels. The war brought a halt to that, although not a total stop - as we will find out. It was, however, the 1950s and the 1960s that saw a huge increase in the Italian population who, almost without exception, went into Jersey's catering industry.

So, what started before the war in the 1930s as a trickle became, in the period of the major expansion of Jersey tourism, a flood. The Italian community in Jersey, although the figures are not clear, grew to the generally accepted level of about 3,000 by the end of the 1960s. Not many of that influx of Italians who became the face of Jersey's catering trade in the golden days of Jersey tourism now remain, but the memories of those who have stayed make up an important part of Jersey's social history - a part that could be forgotten if their memories were not crystallised and preserved.

It is easy to look at Jersey's catering industry and what's left of our hotel industry - as compared to the tourism heyday - and forget that, successful as it seems now, it was as important to the Island then as is the finance industry now, some 60 years later. Tourism was the Island's major industry and an important factor in that rise in status was the Italian community.

The Italians brought a vibrancy as well as knowledge and professionalism to the Island as it did to the larger community of the United Kingdom. Like Jersey, it was still dragging itself out of austerity and, to a degree, was in isolation from developments in catering across the rest of Europe.

In Jersey we needed a new generation of experts to show us the way and that was provided by a host of young men, keen to advance their careers, keen to make something of their lot and so provide a better start for their own families than they thought could be found in post-war Italy. They arrived, many of them, already equipped with the ability to make the catering industry in Jersey the vehicle by which that could be achieved.

It was the 1950s that saw the start of the great Italian invasion of Jersey; they left Italy in their tens of thousands - but why did some of them end up in Jersey? There are various reasons for that as we will see. But Franco Morosino knows well that the story actually goes back to before the war.

He is one of the longer serving Italians in Jersey having been in the Island for more than six decades, arriving here from Asti in Piemonte in 1953. So why did he come to Jersey? And what was the Italy he left behind?

In simple terms, he had already completed his national service and he felt he needed another language if he wished to get a better job anywhere and so improve his chances of success.

He said: 'At that time Italy was like the third world, nothing seemed to happen in the modern way; there was no social security and I used to slave away all day in a little café-restaurant. The work was hard and I am sure, unregulated and outside any published regulations. We would have a break at the times when what we called the Polizia Annonaria, the food distribution inspectorate, announced their inspection. My employers used to send me and one other chap, Augusto, out for a walk so the Annonaria wouldn't see us. It was just as well, therefore, that the inspection was announced well in advance.'

Indeed it was, for there was no chance of Franco's employment conditions meeting any of the official requirements. 'Anyway, that is an illustration of how bad it was. I was paid 1,000 lire a day; at the time, there were about 3,000 lire to the pound.' It is difficult to equate the value of such a sum of money in terms of buying power but, at the time, according to Franco, it was a pretty small wage especially as he worked from opening time until he was allowed to go home.

'It wasn't very much, that was for sure, but to be fair, we ate there and we returned home only to sleep so we got all the food we needed at work. For those who lived out in the country, there was always the chance of augmenting your food stock by growing some extra necessities. You could survive but it was hardly a living wage. Whatever you spent was planned and earmarked well in advance and basically whatever you earned went into the pot as you tried to make ends meet as a family.'

Bruno Zunino is one of the Grand Old Men of Jersey catering: His work here has been recognised by the Italian community with a special award from AMIRA, (the association of Italian head waiters and restaurateurs - see chapter 10), and for the last 30 years or more he has been a partner in La Taverne Restaurant just opposite the Town Hall, Bruno and his colleagues, including Bruno Pesco, created it out of the Cup and Saucer café and which they used to run before upgrading it in the late 1970s.

He comes from St. Remo, a beautiful town on the Italian Riviera, so why did he choose to leave? After all, he was working as a page boy in a big hotel in St. Remo, The Royal, which, since 1872, prided itself on maintaining a past magnificence in a homage to a high baroque fashion that offered luxury rooms and quality cuisine, all set in a sub-tropical mini park, right on the sea front.

The answer is familiar: 'If you were in any way career minded, you needed a language if you were ever going to advance and get a better job,' he said. Obviously he had a head start as, living so near France, he had picked up a certain amount of French. But he needed another language, English.

In 1953 Bruno came to Jersey 'and as any of my long time colleagues here will confirm, life then was better in Jersey than back in Italy, so we stayed. We were making better money and we had more respect for what we did here in Jersey than back in Italy.' Suddenly, he discovered that he wasn't just a page boy, the lowest of the low, but he was treated like a real person and there was something about doing your job which was definitely better: 'It was a friendly atmosphere. Jersey was buzzing with holiday makers and so we stayed. And then of course we met the girls and that gave us even more reason to stay.'

Jersey was a relatively easy choice for Franco Morosino, as was the catering industry as a career. His family contained a fair number who worked, or had worked, in hotels and restaurants; also his uncle, his mother's brother, Pierino, came to the Island in 1938 as a head waiter at the Normandie Hotel on Havre des Pas where he brought a brigade to work for the season. However, the war came, which put a stop to any long term plans to come to the Island. But in 1948 he returned: 'Since that time a lot of people from my part of the world came here through his recommendation or because they knew someone who knew him; you know how the word gets around.

'My sister was married here and I think my grandfather's brother had been here. Anyway my family certainly knew of Jersey since the 1930s so that is one of the reasons I chose to come here.'

Mauro Mori arrived in Jersey when he was 19 and has been in the Island since 1958. Although he was not a waiter with huge experience it was, as he put it, 'solid and good' at a top hotel in Montecatini Terme, a well known and very fashionable spa in Tuscany. The Grand Hotel La Pace imbued in Mauro the disciplines evident in all the young Italians who had started in high quality hotels in Italy. He had learnt, in effect, the correct way of doing things and so brought with him skills that were welcome in Jersey.

He arrived for his first job in Jersey at the Hotel de l'Europe in Mulcaster Street with a particularly smart and well cut dinner jacket that he had brought with him from his previous position in Montecatini. He said he found it a bit embarrassing walking through the hotel after coming down from his room on the top floor; he would create a wonderful impression on the guests who thought, being so smartly turned out, he was someone very important.

'It was understandable,' he said. 'It was, after all, made for the top hotel in Montecatine Terme where only the best was good enough.'

Bruno's Zunino's first job was at a hotel that doesn't exist anymore: the Aberfeldy on Old St John's Road; it has since suffered the same fate as many others and was developed into a block of very pricey flats. It made him a little sad to see his memories being knocked down as he always looked on his time there very fondly. However nice the new buildings are, the soul of the place had changed; what had been there catered for holiday makers. People from England were hesitant and did not have the money to go abroad but were happy to take a chance on travelling as far as Jersey.

'There were lots of hotels, the season got going with honeymoon couples; the Island was very full and the visitors were so friendly. When you served them and they picked up on your accent, they were very approachable and wanted to associate with you and perhaps even offer you a drink after work. We also worked very long hours, yet it was a good time and I enjoyed it.'

As Jersey's tourism industry expanded, the Tourism department adopted the slogan 'Nearer to France, closer to home'. This was not used at the time of Bruno's arrival in Jersey, but the attitude of the visitors he describes pre-empts the campaign that in a sense traded on the English tourists' fear of foreign travel, with its attendant dangers involving funny food and even funnier languages. Jersey definitely appealed to the mass market and there were some very important factors that helped create demand. These days, the absence of those factors means that the hey-day of tourism plenty can never be recreated.

The first was the ferry service, Weymouth in particular, which was owned by British Rail. BR workers had free travel on the national network and the cross-channel ferry to Jersey was part of that network. Thus travel to Jersey, for tens of thousands of potential, and indeed actual, tourists was free. Cost was not a factor.

On top of that there was the British Pay as You Earn (PAYE) tax system, by which all UK employees had their tax deducted at source at a rate based on a code number that fixed their tax deduction and took into account what, if any, tax allowances they were allowed. Single men living at home or in flats got almost no allowances at all, but if they married in the spring right at the end of the tax year, their married man's tax allowance was paid and back dated back to its beginning, in early April of the year before. Money from the state was paid shortly after the wedding and honeymoon, while travel (if you were lucky), was paid for by BR.

Thus, in theory at least, many had their honeymoons if not paid for them, certainly subsidised, by their tax rebate. The soi-disant honeymoon season started the tourism year and as the high season approached, the Island filled to overflowing with constant public appeals, as the Battle of Flowers loomed near, for beds in private houses or anywhere to which tourists arriving without booking could be directed. Many hotels did not have en-suite bathrooms and the buildings were old and often in need of investment. It was too good to last; the tax laws changed and British Rail cut back from the Channel Islands ferry service.

Jersey had a limit set at around 25,000 hotel beds but that was too many when the tide turned with the younger generation who were not so nervous of foreign travel and who were enticed away by guaranteed sun in the new Mediterranean holidays. There they were greeted with newly built (only just built, in some cases) hotels with en suite bedrooms facing the sea with private balconies and filled up by the new breed of super tour operators such as Clarkson's and Thomson's, who offered glamorous locations at what seemed unbelievably cheap package prices.

Jersey's visitors gradually moved on elsewhere thanks to (as Derek Maltwood, a former Director of Hotel L'Horizon put succinctly): 'the help of Sir Frank Whittle, the inventor of the jet engine.'

But before that time, Jersey, with its expanding tourism industry, provided chances of making more money and offered better prospects to the young Italians, who came here during the 1950s and 1960s, of improving themselves. But the Island also provided other advantages as Giancarlo Mattioli recalls. He was just 19 when he arrived in Jersey in 1959 and there was, for him, another powerful reason for leaving Italy. He would have gone anywhere in the world but what gave Jersey a huge advantage in his eyes was that it was the easiest place to get a work permit for him at that time.

Jersey allowed young men in for the season to work at 18, whereas in England the minimum age for a work permit was 21. 'The other reason was that I was about to be called up for military service in Italy and I didn't want to waste 18 months of my life. I wanted to go abroad and ideally it would have been in the UK; in fact, Jersey was completely unknown to me.'

The winter before he came over, he was working in Cortina d'Ampezzo (commonly referred to as Cortina) a town which was, then as now, a very smart ski resort in the heart of the southern Dolomites (the continuation of the Alps) in the Veneto region of North Eastern Italy. There he met a head waiter from Jersey who was recruiting young waiters to go and work with him at the Normandie Hotel.

It is a theme to be taken up later when considering the background of many of the young men who came to Jersey during this period, as Giancarlo was recruited, not by the Normandie Hotel but by the head waiter creating his own brigade. The hotel made the arrangement for the Bailiff's Permit: two waiters were recruited from Cortina; Giancarlo was one of them.

Vittorio Cornaglia's first season in Jersey in 1954 started in a rather theatrical way, as those who remember him at the Lobster Pot and then at his own restaurant the Sea Crest would have expected. He was born and brought up about 10 kilometres from Turin but it was in a hotel on Lake Garda that a barman told him of Jersey where he had a friend who needed staff. So Victor, as everyone in Jersey knows him, went to the Hotel de France in Jersey, but on seeing the service, he said he was sorry he thought it would be more of a smart four or a five star hotel.

However, he was told that the Water's Edge in Bouley Bay was looking for a waiter. Why didn't he try his luck there?

So he took a bus and arrived a few days before the hotel actually opened for the season; he strolled in and saw a painter who, once he discovered he was Italian, greeted him with a terrible insult.

'"Same to you," I said. "I didn't expect to find people so rude in this place."'

The rough looking painter explained that the head waiter Nino had told him it was an everyday greeting. 'I said: "Oh no, it's very rude," and gave him the translation.'

Victor explained he had heard there was a job here so he had come to look at the hotel and apply. The painter was very welcoming and said there were not many people around at the moment but suggested I strolled round and had a look for myself.

'So I went and looked around,' said Victor, 'thinking that the painter seemed to think he owned the place. I looked about and went back to the painter and told him that the place had a lot of possibility, it was wonderfully sited, beautiful view, lovely layout: I would love to work here and I can just imagine it full of people and looking wonderful.'

The head waiter, Nino, appeared and, having been shouted at for putting the wrong words into his mouth, the painter said: 'This young man is the new waiter.'

'Nino took me to one side and I asked who the painter was. He's the owner I was told. That was a new experience for me I had never seen an owner getting his hands dirty in that way.'

Franco Gatti, who most will remember from the Restaurant de la Poste, was working in Milan when a co-worker told him he was off to Jersey for the season. 'So I said: "What is, or where is Jersey?" I was told it was a little island between England and France and I thought to myself "why not?" I thought it could be quite pleasant doing a season somewhere like that.

'When my friend got to The Olwyn Grove he arranged for the management to get a permit and I set off. I didn't realise how long I would be away.'

Franco, from the Barbera region in Piemonte, arrived in Jersey aged 20 in 1961 and started his first job at the Olwyn Grove Hotel (the site is now, Cranham Court) in Mont Millais. He covered breakfast, lunch and dinner and having cleared up the dinner, he was on duty to serve those at the visiting cabaret which toured the hotels - a 14 - hour day.

'These days the manager or owner would be hung up outside the hotel as a warning to others."

The system of the Bailiff's permit continued right though this period as the late Giuseppe Francescon remembered. He was one of the younger generations of Italians who came in 1966 at the height of Jersey's tourism success. He remembered that he didn't choose the Island as he had not an idea as to what, or where, Jersey was. But he received a letter from a friend with whom he had worked at other hotels who, it turned out, was working in Jersey. He fixed on a simple sentence from that letter: 'I'm in Jersey it's a beautiful island, why don't you come and work here?'

As Giuseppe said: 'I thought it would be a good place in which to work as I wanted to learn English. However, my problem had been that I was only 19 years old and so couldn't get a work permit for England until I was 21.'

He didn't mind having to get a permit; it was common practice as every country seemed to have some type of restriction for foreign workers. He said that in Switzerland at the time the story was that everyone working there had to surrender their passport, which could not be reclaimed until you paid your tax and so cleared the way for you to leave:

'True or not, in Jersey those coming to work here had to have the Bailiff's permit.' Giuseppe said: 'It was easy enough to get one it seems, but its conditions were quite restrictive - you couldn't change the essential nature of your job. I couldn't become a window cleaner, I couldn't be a plumber or anything, it had to be a job in the hotel or catering industry, no other type of work was allowed.'

In some countries, regulations are more honoured in their breach than in their observance but Jersey was not one of those. The Bailiff's permit was just for the season, such was the nature of the majority of Jersey's hotels, and you could only stay if you could find winter employment. But as Giuseppe once said, it didn't end there, there were checks to make sure you were still complying with the conditions and there were also health checks.

'Oh yes, every year just down Halkett Place, there was an x-ray screening test. Great lines of us extended down the road from outside that centre; it was like cattle being herded or even the sheep queuing up for the dip. You were checked and if there was anything wrong with you, that was it, you had to leave. That at least was what we were told, but on the other hand I never heard of anyone who was sent home because of that,' he once said in a recorded interview. 'As you can see I wasn't sent home, I am still here.'

Renzo Martin presents the Capo di Stato to Tino Rossi on behalf of the Italian Government, Photo courtesy of Jersey Evening Post

Chapter 2

STAYING ON

THE feature of Jersey life that first hit home for the young Italians coming to Jersey in the 1950s and early 1960s was the Bailiff's Permit. It was helpful inasmuch as it would be issued to men as young as 18, unlike in England where the age was 21. But it was restrictive in what it allowed them to do, and, the fact that it was only issued for a six month period, they were restricted in the length of time they could do it.

Giancarlo Mattioli remembers the permit system that allowed a young man to come to Jersey to work, but as you could only stay as long as you had a permit and were employed, the winter therefore was not easy, as the Bailiff's permit specifically linked you to a type of job.

'We had to stay here in guaranteed employment for eight years before we were free of the constraints of that permit,' he said. 'I managed to achieve that because I stuck to it and went out of my way to find winter employment.'

And like many of his generation, Giancarlo started his working life at an age we would regard as impossibly young. When he came to Jersey, he was one of a large community of at least a couple of thousand, possibly. This was quite a noticeable influx into a small community.

'I started working in the catering industry at the age of 11 - part time, obviously, because I also had to go to school. I left school at 14 and started to work full time so, by the time I came to Jersey at 19, it was as an assistant restaurant manager. I stood in for a time as head waiter at the Pomme d'Or at the age of 21, as by then I had clocked up a lot of experience. I wasn't afraid of responding to the demands of customers and being nice to them and politely supplying what they needed - it came fairly easily to me. If we Italians weren't actually born with those skills, we certainly had them drummed into us from an early age.'

But by the middle 1960s, towards the end of the big influx of Italians in the early 1970s, the younger generation still came to Jersey as the word had got out that the Island was worth coming to. Eric Ruaro remembers when, back in 1965, he was in the catering trade working away from his home in the very north of Italy near Lake Maggiore. He had got a job at the ski resort of Madonna di Campiglio in the Brenta Dolomites in the North East, a small yet highly regarded resort for the quality of its skiing.

He remembers being back at home for a short break when he met a friend who had come back home on a holiday from Jersey, who suggested he came over. 'I got a bit carried away with the idea, I must admit,' he remembers. 'The next thing I knew I had managed to arrange both a contract of employment and a permit. I was rather concerned as reality struck home, as I had to go to the hotel manageress - a big Austrian lady with red hair, I recall - and tell her that I would like to leave in March to get to Jersey for the start of the summer season. This was despite the fact that I had signed a contract through to April.' In the event she agreed but, as a bit of advice for the future, told young Eric to remember the two most important words in English he would ever need: 'self-control'. He says they were the first two English words he learnt.

There were quite a few people from his part of Italy already in Jersey, for the Lakes region of Piemonte was an area that supplied many people into the catering trade.

'Oh yes, there were quite a few from that region; in fact there was a local joke that when you have a very young baby boy, you get him to clasp on a thin bar or a huge nail in the wall. If he hangs on, or even starts to pull himself up, he will be a chef; otherwise he will become a waiter.

'Presumably I managed to hang on and was a trainee chef to start with, but I was offered a job in the dining room in Jersey so I became a waiter. Frankly it gave me an opportunity to travel and I had a good offer, so it didn't make any difference to me one way or the other.'

Also from the same part of the world as Eric, although a little higher up in the Alps, is Paulo Crolla who hails from Domodossola situated on the way up to the Simplon Pass. The town acts as a minor passenger-rail hub. Its strategic location accommodates Swiss rail passengers and Domodossola railway station acts as an international stopping-point between Milan and Switzerland. Of the generation of successful Italians who came to Jersey in this period, Paulo is one of the youngest. In fact he is still working, having had his own restaurant that closed at the end of a lease. After a gap when he considered retiring, but not being able to accept doing nothing, he became the maître d'hôtel at the St Brelade's Bay.

He was also working in the Dolomites at a ski resort - and this is becoming a familiar story. It just happened that one of his colleagues worked in Jersey every season and he was choosing a brigade and therefore picking the best of what he could find.

'And so that brought me here to Jersey.' That was to the Normandie Hotel and the man who bought him over had been coming to Jersey for the previous 25 years, just for the season. Wherever he worked in the winter, he used to form his own brigade and take it across to Jersey for the season. 'So it just so happened that I was there and I came across. Quite simply it was not a choice I really made; it was just a question of being in the right place at the right time.'

Maurizio Marzana arrived here in 1971 and is still working in the trade, being a part owner of the *Bon Viveur* in St Aubin. Before he came to Jersey he had been working at some of the top hotels in Europe and was already established as a well paid professional. He had worked in the Grand Hotel Regina in the Jungfrau Region of Switzerland, what is now called the Bellevue Palace in Berne and also in the Maritim Hotel, Timmendorfer Strand, in Northern Germany on the Baltic coast. Then after a season there and being head of a station of ten tables, he decided he had to learn English to progress any further up the ladder to become a maître d'hôtel.

'I wanted to improve my English, or perhaps learn English would be more truthful, and one of the waiters there had worked in Jersey at the Atlantic Hotel and he suggested going there.' Maurizio applied to two or three brigades and got a job with Aldo Valli, the maître d'hôtel at L'Horizon. So, from Hamburg, he took a train to Paris and then to St Malo before finally arriving in Jersey on the Condor hydrofoil in 1971.

He vividly remembers his arrival in the Island: 'After the endless journey I remember that taxi ride to L'Horizon. The driver was dressed in a very English manner with a light khaki jacket. He kept the window open and continued to make all those complicated hand signals while driving - I thought at the time - very slowly, keeping within the Jersey speed limit.

'This was very strange to me as I come from Italy where no one signals their intentions and where everyone drives as fast as they can. Anyway, to my mind, we crawled along the Esplanade and Victoria Avenue looking at that lovely blue sea but, of course on the wrong side of the road. It was all so different I have never forgotten it, and it kept me chuckling for some time. And then the final touch was coming into St Brelade's Bay with the Hotel L'Horizon looking so beautiful in that setting. It was outstanding and the sort of thing that always remains in your mind.'

Maurizio and others, who, like him, arrived comparatively late in the period of the Italian immigration to Jersey, were fortunate in the sense that the word about jobs in the Island's tourism sector had got out. He had, at least, heard of the Island and knew, slightly, to what sort of place he would be going. He was able, given his background, to apply directly to a maître d'hôtel in Jersey to seek a place in his brigade, rather than being recruited by the brigade and then moving to Jersey.

He said he used to keep a book of the top hotels and the best known maîtres, and therefore the best brigades to whom he could apply. He explained that he needed to make sure his career kept on track with good up-to-date references that would give proof of his good training and experience.

A decade and a half earlier it had been, for many, much more a jump into the dark, as was the case, for example, with Mirto Sappé who came to Jersey in 1957. His name became known to a whole generation of diners during his time as restaurant and hotel manager of (and therefore synonymous with) The Moorings in Gorey - but that was in the future. He had been brought up in the very north western corner of Italy, nearly in France; so near to it, in fact, that he and many in his region were bi-lingual. To be even more distinctive, the region - a cluster of valleys known as the Waldencian Valleys - was, and remains, staunchly Protestant.

Mirto had been working in Turin for the previous three years before he came to Jersey. Before that he had completed his catering college course in Florence and then got a job in Turin and at one of that city's top hotels, The Turin Palace, where he was put in reception. He had reached the stage where he could have got the job as the deputy concierge, which, in a big city hotel is quite an exalted position in its own way.

'The head concierge was about to retire and the deputy concierge had been waiting about 20 years for the top job. I was told that if I learnt English (and don't forget I was already, because of my upbringing, bilingual in French and spoke some German) I would be next in line for his position. So I came to Jersey with the intention of learning English and going back to Turin, but it is just as well things worked out differently for, although it was a safe job, it was dead man's shoes in terms of advancement, and the chances are I would have been in the Turin Palace until I retired.'

Mirto came to a small hotel in St Helier, La Corona, which he described as 'a lovely typical second register family oriented hotel of the 1950s, where the guests were amazingly good natured and frankly very tolerant.' There were no jobs in reception so he worked in the dining room but, such was the nature of the hotel that everyone, staff and guests, joined in on Battle of Flowers day. 'We were there for the guests all day and they even helped us prepare the packed lunch for later. When we came back from the Battle we gave them a quick dinner and then all went back out together to enjoy the fête. There was, as I said, a lovely family feel to the whole place.'

Mirto was only there for the season, as then the hotel (being strictly seasonal) closed down for the winter. He was lucky to get a job at the Moorings Hotel in Gorey, which was then one of the Island's top restaurants and very profitable for the owners as well as for the staff, as they were very busy.

Having a job for the winter meant Mirto's Bailiff's permit could be extended: 'And then I met my wife the following spring and that was that; I never went back to live or work in Italy.'

There are many coincidences in the careers of the Italians who came to Jersey and the somewhat unlikely combination of La Corona Hotel, the Moorings and the Turin Palace crops up again as Mirto's short stay was not the last La Corona saw of Italians from the North West during the 1950s.

Renzo Martin, for many years the Italian Consular Agent for the Channel Islands, also started in Jersey at La Corona. His English, he explained, was pretty basic but he had learned some at school and it was good enough to be a barman in Jersey. Coincidentally, he had learnt a bit more as he also worked for a time at the Turin Palace and, as his French was also very good, he was offered Mirto's job when he left to go to Jersey.

In fact Mirto Sappé had suggested he should try Jersey as La Corona needed more staff and the hotel also needed a chef. So one of the second chefs from the Turin Palace, Settimo (Setti) Pozzi, came to work in the kitchen and Renzo came as a barman. His 'extra job' was to translate for Setti in the kitchen. But there was a problem: Setti was already a good Salon Culinaire chef and he had been working at the Turin Palace, which was a five star hotel in one of Italy's principal cities. The Corona was more meat and two veg. Setti had suddenly to unlearn some of what he knew and then learn how to make such delicacies as shepherd's pie and steamed pudding.

In the event he just could not, or would not, do it and managed instead to become employed at the Moorings Hotel as second chef; Renzo was also to become the general manager of a group that purchased the hotel. But going back to earlier times, Renzo said that Setti was in a good position as The Moorings stayed open in the winter. 'I almost got myself a job at the Ommaroo Hotel as a kitchen porter after the Corona closed for the winter. Actually, I had hoped to get a job in Zurich. I had gone back home and paid my Father back the money he had lent me to get to Jersey; having done that, I eventually changed my mind and decided to come back here.'

The Ommaroo at Havre des Pas is a collection of terrace houses merged together over the years to make a long lived and successful family-run hotel that recently celebrated its centenary. The problem had always been that each of the individual houses still has its old staircase *in situ* and the room numbers were assigned as the hotel gradually expanded sideways and added another house from the terrace. Back then, there appeared to be no rhyme or reason to the room numbering system. There was a story that the hotel is haunted by a guest who went up one of the many staircases to his room, never to be seen again other than as a spectral presence. Apparently, like the ghost ship, the *Flying Dutchman*, forever seeking a port, the ghost of the Ommaroo guest is destined to remain forever looking for his room.

Mauro Mori quickly made his presence felt at the Hotel de l'Europe in Mulcaster Street. 'There was a time when the head waiter fell out with the boss and got the sack and so we then had two or three waiters doing the job when they could and the results were terrible: no system, no control, nothing.

'One day I just put my foot down and said: "Come on, we must do things properly - we cannot carry on like this". At least, I said, we should have a dining room plan with the number of the table and the name of those on it, because with no system, the receptionist or someone from the office had to go round to see who was having what and therefore what to charge for extras.'

The manager thought for a second, adopted the system and the next year Mauro was made head waiter at the age of 21.

Franco Gatti

A youthful Angelo Mariani

Franco Morosino

Angelo Mariani (far right) with the family at the centre of the immigration row in 1961. Guido Parmisani his brother-in-law, Palmira Mariani, his sister, and his niece Anna

Not long married. Giancarlo and Antonietta Mattioli at Snow Hill, St Helier

Giancarlo and Antonietta Mattioli, setting off together to the Mecca Function Rooms in Tottenham, Court Road, London

Franco Gatti

Frank Berni, founder of Berni Inns and a public benefactor in Jersey

Giuseppe Ferri at the Bel Sit Cafe

Mirto Sappé, manager of the Moorings Hotel, Gorey Pier

Maurizio Marzana (seated 3rd from right)
with his brigade at the Grand Hotel c.1979

Italian Food Fair: left to right: Victor Cornaglia, Renzo Martin,
Giuseppe Francescon, Giovanni Venticinque, Sandro Tiboni

Giuseppe Francescon, receiving career advice from HM The Queen in 1989

Giancarlo Mattioli during his time at the Pomme d'Or

Giuseppe Francescon, Piero Guglieri, Sandro Tiboni

Italian dancers including one very young Philippa clutching her mother's hand Serafina Venticinque (right). Also on the left, Angela Venticinque and Maria Carla Farina (2nd from Left)

Piero Guglieri, Giacommo Pini,
Giuseppe Francescon and two bowls of zabaglioni

Angela & Serafina Venticinque at the Italian Food Fair,
Halkett Place in 1988 with, on the right, Maria Carla Farina

Angelo Mariani was for many years a familiar figure in the centre of St Helier, running the highly successful Gimbels Restaurant in Colomberie and then taking over as an owner of the Steak House at Charing Cross. His time in Jersey started at the Hotel de France in 1955 where he was a kitchen porter, which he chose because 'my brother-in-law was a second chef there and he was living in Jersey with my sister Palmira'.

And another of the type of coincidence that is rife among the Jersey Italians, Angelo is from same area of Italy (a small area in the region of Lazio), as Maurizio Marzana. In fact their families only live a few kilometres away in the province of Frosinone, near Rome.

Although some of Angelo's compatriots got a permit to avoid the compulsory military service on the basis of being a family earner and being fully employed in another country (or just keeping below the official radar), he decided on a simpler approach. So, rather than having an official limit imposed on the number of days that he would be allowed to stay in Italy in a given year, he would join up.

He was already past his official call-up date as he had gone to England to see if he could find any jobs for the winter. 'I had gone to Liverpool with a friend and then made my way back to London stopping off, it seemed, at every town on the way, but there was nothing for me. Finally I decided, frankly, that it was almost easier to do the military service for just over a year rather than face some sort of official hassle from the authorities for years and years and so never be able to go and see my family when I wanted.'

So he took a train back to Italy from London (six months late for call up) and when he got to Ventimiglia Station at the Italian border the Carabinieri took his passport. 'Four days later I was in a uniform starting my military service. The USA and Russia appeared to be in a permanent standoff in those days and then Kennedy was assassinated just before I was due to be discharged. Worried about what would happen, the Army extended the term of service and it was 18 months before I got out.'

Despite being caught up in the military for longer than he intended, perhaps Angelo had a point. Paulo Crolla had been in Jersey for two years before he decided to try and sort out his standing by going through the proper channels. He went to see the Consular Agent, who was, at that time, Luigi Forte, and explained his position; he was then given a couple of documents to sign. 'Luigi told me that whenever I wanted to go to Italy

I had to notify him and he would give me a permit, duly stamped and I then had show it to the local Carabinieri when I got home.

'Once in Italy, they would then stamp it, visit the house to check that was where I was really going and, when I told them I was leaving, it would be stamped again and they would then come out to the house once more after I was due to leave and check if I had really gone. That went on for years and years and always, when I went to see my parents, the Carabinieri would always pop up later to ask: "Has he gone?" Now it is all different, but back then I was only allowed to be in Italy for a maximum of three months a year. '

It was no ordinary police force that picked up Angelo and, in effect, dropped him in the Army and also checked up every time Paulo returned home. It was the Carabinieri, which is the national gendarmerie of Italy, policing both military and civilian populations. It started as the police force of the Kingdom of Sardinia but during the process of Italian unification, it was appointed the 'First Force' of the new national military organisation.

Also to be found around St Helier in the late 1950s was Giovanni Venticinque. He has been deeply involved in the Italian community since the early days for, as well as being an organiser of the Italian Club, he was also president of the Circolo Italiano for many years. He came from the small town of Leonfort in region of Catania, in Sicily: He wasn't the only person to leave; the level of emigration from that town resulted in another Leonfort emerging in Argentina.

April 1957 was the year when he arrived in Jersey after a spell in the army, which he had joined in 1949. There he had gained experience in a variety of disciplines and skills, including running a kitchen where he had a brigade of 42. He was based north of Venice, at the City of Udine in the Friuli, where he met Maria. There came the time when he planned to leave the service and return to his native Sicily, but the pair decided to stay together and she became his wife. He could hardly have chosen a spouse at a greater distance from his home town who was yet still Italian. So the newly married young man needed regular work and luckily, three years later, after a chance letter from Jersey penned by an old friend from his army days, 'it was not too long before Maria and I were in Jersey'.

Also from Sicily came Angelo Saccone, a familiar face in St Helier's King Street, as he was the manager of two well known shops for much of his working life; the leather goods shop Holts and later, manager of the shoe shop Saxone. Born and brought up in Palermo, he attended the catering school there for four years: 'I had big ideas - I wanted to learn languages and end up as a hotel manager. French was a compulsory language, English was not. I tried to learn it but found it very difficult as there appeared to be no fixed rules.'

But fate was going to take him out of Italy. After the last summer at catering school he found a job as a trainee in Lido di Jessolo in the Province of Venice; then, as now, a beach resort famous for its 15 kilometres of sand, with each hotel fronting the sea and having its own private section of beach with tables, umbrellas and sun loungers. There Angelo met many English tourists and families (and of course the girls) and decided that was where he wanted to go.

'Then I found out about the age limit for an English work permit so instead I was found a place in the Isle of Man. After a month the hotel went bankrupt and I felt I had gone all that way for nothing.'

Nevertheless, he had a contact in Birmingham who had been to Jersey, worked at the Steak House and had kept in touch with Franco Morosino who had worked in Jersey since the early 1950s. 'Franco introduced me to Italo Miorin, the head waiter at the Pomme d'Or and soon I was employed there and stayed for five years.'

Angelo, as well as Mirto Sappé, Renzo Martin and Angelo Mariani, were examples of those who came to Jersey by relying on introductions from family or contacts, or who came just out of perseverance and the desire to find somewhere where they could improve their lot. Many, however, were recruited by, or applied to join, specific brigades. Tino Rossi of La Capannina is a case in point. When he started in the business, he didn't really choose to work anywhere specifically; he wanted to work abroad and chose any brigade that he was able to join. When he wanted to move on, he opted for a brigade in Jersey.

So to a young man setting out on his career it wasn't the best hotel that was the prime factor, rather it was a good maître d'hôtel to whom you attached yourself. You looked for the best man available who would take you on, according to Tino, like a young ambitious footballer following the best manager.

‘Yes, you would try very hard to get into the best brigade you could find and that meant applying to the best maître d’hôtel you could approach. And the better, the more elite, the brigade that you could find meant that you had greater opportunities to advance and improve your prospects and thus your career in general.’

As Tino remembers, the different stages of that career were very long in those days. ‘For example, if you wanted to become a chef de rang or a sommelier within a few years, you had to work very hard. Commis, demi-chef de rang, chef du rang, you had to work your way through the system and maybe someone would drop out of the brigade and you could step up to the vacant position. It was all down to hard work and developing your skills.’

So in a sense, Tino, as was the case with many others, didn’t really choose to come to Jersey. He chose to work abroad and chose a brigade that he managed to join. For some, that brigade made Jersey a destination.

As a young man, Tino was working in Switzerland in a brigade that he had joined for experience and to learn foreign languages. Learning English proved a problem in those days, because of the well-nigh impossibility of getting a permit to work in England if you were under 21.

Tino remembers: ‘You could organise an approved work exchange or work in an embassy if you had the connections, but it was much easier, to come to Jersey, as those who came in those times have confirmed, for you could get a seasonal permit at the age of 18. ‘In my case the permit was issued by the Hotel L’Horizon, which made all the arrangements; however, in my mind I was employed, not so much by the hotel, but by the brigade run by Giuseppe Panigarda.’

The Hotel L'Horizon, which now gives the impression of a mid-20th century building, has its origins back in the previous century. Derek Maltwood, a director of the hotel in the 1970s and 1980s, remembers stories of the building’s history. The White House, the original building standing where the Hotel L’Horizon now is, belonged to the owners of St John’s Manor who used it as a beach house. Apparently in Edwardian days, the family used to migrate there for the summer holidays. It would be heralded by a convoy of carts with staff bringing the necessities for an extended stay of a couple of months, then a cavalcade of carriages with matching yellow wheels would announce the arrival of the family.

But it was Associated Hotels, under the chairmanship of George Francis Child Villiers, the ninth Earl of Jersey that, in the 1950s, developed the property into a hotel for the first time. The company also owned the Star Restaurant in St Helier and the dining rooms of both establishments saw the start of many successful careers for Italians coming to Jersey.

Furthermore, it was in Hotel L'Horizon that the dual reign of Piero Alzetta in the kitchen and Aldo Valli in the dining room, maintained the pre-eminent position of the hotel in the group consciousness of the Island for so long and, in so doing, drip-fed the Island with Italian talent.

Derek Maltwood recalls that neither the manager, John Wileman, nor any of the directors, were allowed in the kitchen without the approval of Piero Alzetta. 'It was his domain and that was it. Furthermore, Aldo Valli made it as essential as much as he could, not to allow any waiter loose on the hotel guests without first getting the young man to serve him an entire meal correctly, and to his satisfaction. Furthermore, an ability to speak some English was essential.'

Whether they arrived with advanced skills or used Jersey as a base to develop them, whether they came to learn English, whether they arrived in a brigade or joined one on their arrival, there was one thing that united all the Italians who came here. They wanted to get on in the world and achieve something which would have been impossible at home, given the economic situation in their own country.

But they were also young men far from home and in a strange country. There was a lot to learn and they had to get used to the many differences and, above all, learn to adapt.

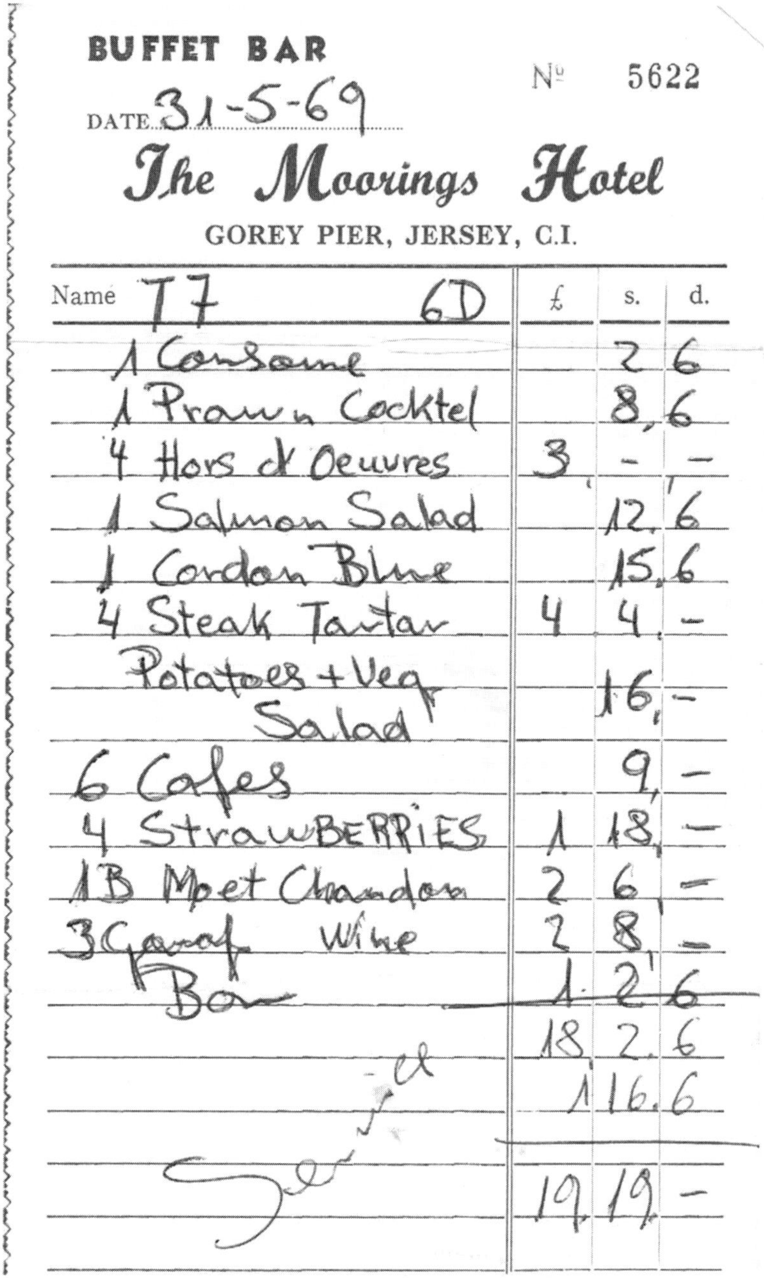

BUFFET BAR

№ 5622

DATE 31-5-69

The Moorings Hotel

GOREY PIER, JERSEY, C.I.

Name T7 6D	£	s.	d.
1 Consomme		2	6
1 Prawn Cocktel		8	6
4 Hors d'Oeuvres	3	–	–
1 Salmon Salad		12	6
1 Cordon Blue		15	6
4 Steak Tartar	4	4	–
Potatoes + Veg Salad		16	–
6 Cafes		9	–
4 StrawBERRIES	1	18	–
1B Moet Chandon	2	6	–
3 Caraf Wine	2	8	–
Bar	1	2	6
	18	2	6
Service	1	16	6
	19	19	–

Lunch at The Moorings 1969; just over £3 per head and no holding back.

Chapter 3

SETTLING IN

THERE were thousands of Italians who came to Jersey in the 1950s and 1960s; some say that there were around 3,000 living and working in the Island. The total number remains at best a guestimate until, that is, someone can find their way into the consular archives in London, blow away the dust and count up all the appropriate pieces of paper.

Be that as it may, circumstances changed, horizons widened, the up-and-coming cruise industry beckoned and there was also the call of home back in Italy - especially an Italy that was turning the corner economically. That call was strong and for that - or a combination of any, or all, of these reasons - many left.

Staying or leaving, originally they had arrived in Jersey for similar reasons: they were anxious to earn better money and at the same time learn English to advance their careers. Some wanted to avoid military service and for others Jersey had the advantage because they could come here and get a work permit at a younger age than in the UK.

Those who elected to stay blended into Jersey society very quickly and, apparently, very easily. Jersey was fortunate to have them for, stay or leave, they all helped contribute to the establishment and expansion of the post-war tourism and catering industry. They brought with them professionalism based on a strong training ethic and so helped open up the Island to developments, not only in catering, but also in the method of service from outside Jersey, as well as outside the United Kingdom.

It was a crucial couple of decades for Jersey Tourism and the memories of those Italians, who came here and chose to stay, make up an important part of Jersey's social history. This is a chapter of a long history which, in an ideal world, would be an overall view of the change in Jersey society over the centuries that had been brought about by shifts in the make-up of the indigenous population. It will, no doubt, be fully researched and written up one day by a dedicated and professional social historian. Meanwhile we have many a witness - yesterday's witnesses (to adapt the title of an excellent BBC radio series) - to an element of this story. They were participants who look back at this period as they remember it; others will have different memories.

But for them it starts with their arrival to these shores and the realisation, for those young hopefuls who came looking for a better life, that they were far from home and had to adapt to a very different world from the one they had left behind.

When the first wave of this generation of Italians arrived in the early 1950s, young men such as Bruno Zunino, Franco Morosino and others of that cohort who came to work in the catering trade, discovered that, in terms of food and what was on offer, Jersey was very different and was quite simply a total change from what they saw as normal. It was still a time of what they perceived as strange dining room practices, remnants of which continued well into the 1970s, and of uninspired catering, where in some hotels, a small glass of fruit juice was considered perfectly adequate to offer as a starter.

Bruno Zunino recalls that, when he arrived in the early 1950s, there was still a feeling of post-war austerity and for some time, variety was not a strong feature of the average hotel dining room menu: 'I remember that the most popular, and therefore universally available, dishes being served in some hotel restaurants were potted shrimps, prawn cocktail, steak and kidney pudding, roast beef, roast lamb - and that was about it.'

Gradually that changed and as foreign staff began taking over the kitchens and dining rooms, they could provide greater choice for those guests and visitors who had acquired some experience of a more international cuisine. Bruno recalls the foreign chefs who came to Jersey: 'There were Italians, and there were some excellent German chefs too, and gradually the offerings on the menu became more what the English might call adventurous. Certainly there was more variety.'

For many Italians it was the lack, on arrival, of what they would have considered basic materials that was the most surprising - indeed the most disconcerting - discovery. If they wanted to make an Italian dish there was, for example, no olive oil readily available; pasta was difficult to find; tinned tomatoes a rarity; tomato concentrate impossible to obtain; in fact there was almost nothing available in those days from their own land that might remind them of home; nothing to cling to as some form of consolation to ease the homesickness.

And although the catering suppliers started to respond to the changing demand, this did not percolate through the system into general retail until much later. Angelo Saccone, who came to Jersey from Sicily much later, in 1970, recalls the time, soon after he arrived, when he developed an earache which kept on returning just when he thought it had gone away: 'I remember mentioning in a letter home that I had this problem with a recurring earache and my mother replied, by return (that's mothers for you!) telling me to get a bit of olive oil, warm it up in a spoon and put a little in my ear and I would soon be all right.'

As he said, for an Italian - a Sicilian woman at that - getting olive oil would be as easy as turning on a tap. But in Jersey? Not so simple: 'I eventually found some at Le Quesne's chemists. My mother thought it would be easy for me to pop into the nearest corner shop.'

Franco Morosino remembers his surprise at the long list of what he couldn't get when he arrived in Jersey in the early 1950s: 'You couldn't get Parma ham, you couldn't get olive oil, you couldn't get parmesan cheese… then slowly it started coming in. I think Luigi Forte tried to import some products from Italy as he had a couple of café-restaurants, and then the commercially savvy Italians living in England obviously realised there was money to be made for they had started UK-based import firms bringing over wines and other produce and so we could bring it into Jersey from there.'

And then the subject turned to wines, those which Bruno and Franco remembered as being available in the shops and what turned up on wine lists. 'At one time,' said Franco, 'it seemed the most popular - indeed it seemed the only - wines in Jersey were cheap Sauternes and Barsac and of course Liebfraumilch.' (Mateus Rose had yet to conquer the world.)

That basic list soon included Chianti (in a flask of course - it couldn't be sold otherwise; for some time, it almost seemed that if a bottle did not appear in a straw flask it just couldn't be Italian). Even wines that were good products in Italy - Soave and Valpolicella Classico for example - were diminished in people's eyes by appearing in large 2 litre bottles, to be sold off at the cheapest price possible.

Franco remembers those times: 'After a few years the first of us started opening our own little cafés and restaurants and they had to get the proper stuff in to produce some authentic dishes and so the London-based Italian traders put Jersey on their list of prospects and the products started arriving.'

Even in this field the Jersey Italian connection was strong for, by the late 1970s, one ex-member of the Italian community in Jersey had become a major force in the London wine trade. Renato Trestini became a passionate advocate for quality Italian wines; he started importing them in a small way and gradually built up business and, above all, influence. From the mid 1970s onwards he was frequently being quoted in wine columns and specialist wine magazines for recommendations, not only on what to drink, but also suggestions as to which wine to serve with a variety of dishes, not just those made from Italian recipes.

His connections in Italy gave him access to quality products from all round the country and soon his wines were being imported by Mirto Sappé's own company, Gorey Wine Company. By the early 1980s wines from the top to the toe of Italy - many sourced through Renato - were also being imported by Merchant Vintners, the Jersey wine wholesalers. One of the founder directors of that company was Eric Ruaro (whom we met in Chapter One) who came to Jersey from near Lake Maggiore in 1965; and I was the other founder.

As a young man in a strange country, Eric, as so many others, came here to learn English and so improve his career prospects. He took lessons but quickly realised, as did many of his compatriots, that language could be learnt best by consciously joining the community or, to put it another way, integrating. He said that he was not alone in making a point of not immersing himself too much in the Italian community and so distanced himself from it very quickly, as did others, perhaps many of those who have stayed: 'I don't want to exaggerate that point, but I knew there was a bigger world outside. I had three English lessons and then I made a point of seeing English films at the cinema and I was also very lucky with my life here, as I had English (or Jersey) friends and acquaintances, all of whom had a very good command of their language and, by mixing with them, my English improved very very fast.'

Renzo Martin, early in his career, was barman at the Links Hotel and one of the customers there was Peter Rendle, now a retired architect. He recalls Renzo facing a problem that was by no means unique among the Italians living in Jersey; the English had trouble with Italian names. Peter remembers the owner could never understand that her barman's name was Renzo, not Lorenzo.

Renzo laughed at the memory. 'That's true, Mrs Le Sueur always called me Lorenzo and very politely I said to her, each time she got it wrong (and that was every time she talked to me): "My name is not Lorenzo, Mrs Le Sueur, but Renzo."

'"Yes, Lorenzo," she would say, and carry on as before.'

One summer, he remembered the tips were not as good as he had hoped and so he resorted to humour to encourage a bit more giving. He used an empty Dimple Haig whisky bottle which would fit sixpences down the neck and stood it in the bar with a sign saying: 'For Lorenzo's holidays in Italy - fed up with blondes, want some brunettes.' It was a very obvious joke with no intention to deceive.

'All the ladies used to come in to the bar; look at the notice have a chuckle and put a sixpence in.' He remembers that when the bottle started filling up he put it on top of the big fridge and let the vibrations do their work gradually and so, over a few days, the sixpences started to settle and leave more space. 'One morning Mrs Le Sueur came in and said: "Oh, Lorenzo" (that name again) "you've been at the bottle, or someone's been stealing your sixpences."'

Giuseppe Ferri, to most of the Italian community, was one of the faces of the Bel Sit café at the top of Bath Street and so occupied a central role in the leisure time of the community, many of whom would pop in for a coffee and a gossip when the opportunity presented itself. But that is a story for later.

He arrived in 1957 from Piacenza in the Emilia Romagna but he had worked at the Palace Hotel in Milan. However, his demi-chef de rang at the hotel went to Jersey and later wrote to suggest it would be a useful place for him to come and learn English; so he came just for one season to get, at least, the basics of the language.

'I was lucky,' he said. 'I was working in The Royal Hotel and, come the winter, the manager said I could stay. He told me I would be fed and be given a bed and paid when there was work; I didn't go back to Italy that winter. Although I was technically only a commis, I was a waiter like anyone else because the service in the Royal was pretty easy and straight forward. Not having any English, I wasn't working in the ballroom at night so I was always on afternoon tea when I first arrived.'

Sticking in his mind from those days are memories of St Helier and, if there was a function at the Royal and he was not required until perhaps later on to help with the clearing up, he used to go into town.

'And heading back later, there were still gas lights to guide me. There were not many left and I remember one being at top of Bath Street near where the Bel Sit was to be, one near the old Jersey Evening Post building on the corner of Charles Street and one by the chemist, De Faye's. It seemed so strange to see them still being used. But they were valuable to me for they were turned off at 11.00pm, I seem to remember, and that was a message to me that I was running late.'

According to Franco Gatti, the Italians settled in quickly and did well when they arrived because there was no real competition. The Jersey people, he reckoned, were good at many things but not at being waiters. 'They didn't want to do it so we had an open market waiting to be filled. In Italy we might not have done as well, as there was much more competition.'

He said that even the successful restaurateurs, Tino Rossi, for example at La Capannina (who was and who remains an excellent restaurateur), had another advantage of not having too much competition. 'When we came there were no Italian restaurants, no large body of waiters, that's what I mean about an easy market for us. Eating fish and chips out of newspapers is no competition.

'So what I am trying to say is that it was not because the Italians were cleverer than other groups but that those who stayed, survived and did quite well. At that time it was our speciality and no one else was doing it. That is a bit of a generalisation, but you know what I mean.'

As we discovered, Franco Morosino was introduced to Jersey by his uncle who ran a brigade at the Normandie Hotel in the 1930s before the war. But there were others who had seen those times. Bruno Zunino talked of the Italians who were here pre-war, many at the Palace Hotel, now long gone, but the name remains in Palace Close off Bagatelle Road. There were a few who tried to stay on but after the outbreak of hostilities some, Luigi Forte for example, were deported to England.

After the war, Luigi and others in the same position came back to Jersey as soon as it was possible. Luigi was first cousin to Charles Forte who was to become head of the immensely successful UK-based hotel family. They were born in the same village, Montfort, and according to Renzo Martin, the story goes they even shared the same cradle.

Another, of this group, very well known in the 1950s and 1960s, was John Gay, a man who comes into many Italians' early experiences of Jersey. According to Renzo Martin, Gay is an Italian name and John was in Jersey before and during the war. When Italy signed a separate peace agreement with the allied powers, he became - like the rest of Jersey - part of the occupied population and was even interned for a while. After the war he became a naturalised British subject, kept the name Gay but changed his Italian name Giovanni, into the English equivalent, John.

In the 1950s he bought a building that was to become the Savoy Hotel and transformed that relatively small property into a thriving business that became a chosen place for many Italians to work. They were kept busy the year round, as the Savoy became a very popular place for annual dinners and other functions.

Giuseppe Ferri looks back on those early days with pleasure. He recalls the time when he worked at The Continental Hotel in St Saviour's Road, now Liberation Court. 'I tell you something, it was a beautiful life; you worked hard right from the start. It was a hard slog but after an early morning start, at 3.30am, there was time off and I used to go and play football; I was in the hotel team and we won a cup one year that was presented to us by Senator Krichefski. Then it was back in the evening for the dinner service and every other night you were in the ballroom until one o'clock in the morning.'

According to Giuseppe, when he talks of those early days he gets a feeling of pity from some listeners who feel sorry for the hard life he must have had. In a sense they were right, but he doesn't need or want any pity. As he said, it was the way of the world and you accepted it: 'I actually enjoyed it because the company was there, the friendship was there and the respect was there from the manager and that was lovely. It more than made up for the hard work.'

Of course (and we heard it many times from all those we met) most of the Italians came here with the stated intention to increase their prospects by learning English. However, that learning process could cause its own problems in the early days and as Franco Morosino remembers 'could give us all something to laugh about'.

He tells of a friend who went to the one shop patronised by most Italians in their first few days. It was largely self-service, so language was not an issue and so, there in Woolworth's, all could get by without much more than please and thank you: 'In fact, it was memories of those days that made me very sad when the shop closed.'

His friend was looking for some essentials including shaving soap, toothpaste and some form of aftershave. 'Anyway, he bought them and next day came to work and his face was shiny - you could see him coming for miles - and he was also complaining about the toothpaste he had bought which he said tasted awful. I had a closer look and his toothpaste was shaving cream in a tube and the so-called aftershave was brilliantine.'

According to Franco, that sort of thing was not uncommon and it reminded them all of one of the reasons for coming to Jersey, 'to learn English and improve our prospects.' These frequent problems encouraged everyone to find some school that could teach English. It was not exactly a pleasure and indeed has been described as a bit of a torture after a long day's work. 'It was difficult for us to pronounce certain words, but it had to be done. We were here in an English speaking country and you had to learn to fit in. You can't sit in a corner with your friends speaking Italian, and not adapting, instead of trying to integrate.'

That last sentence is telling and it is a theme to which we will return as we follow the way that this generation of Italians has merged into society over the years. But, that said, it wasn't just our language, English, that the Italians learnt, they also taught: they responded by teaching Jersey the grammar and language of Italian cooking and it didn't take too long for the Island to take up that offer. Indeed there are those who remember that era who have said that the Italians taught Jersey, and in particular the Jersey tourism industry, how to eat.

Maybe that is true, maybe it is overstating the case, but what was certainly true is that their presence encouraged the importation of special foods and wines and opened up the tourist trade here in Jersey to influences and familiarity with what was available from Europe that, up to that time, had only been experienced by a privileged few.

As Franco and Bruno both recalled, that view was correct but only to a degree, as there was certainly no conscious effort to create some cult of catering missionaries. To put it at its most basic, they were Italians far from home and they wanted some of their own food such as, for example, Prosciutto di Parma. But Franco recalls some unexpected cultural exchanges: '*Bagna càuda* for example; I would never have thought it would catch on in England. The basic ingredients are garlic, anchovies and olive oil and it is a great speciality and favourite from North West Italy where I come from. But I never would have thought it would be popular here. But we had those dishes for ourselves and the word got out and there are plenty of such examples.'

Bagna càuda; the name, if translated into English from the Piedmontese dialect, would become - "hot dip". It is a warm sauce typical of that region with numerous local variations. Traditionally served and consumed in a manner similar to fondue, it is made with garlic, anchovies, olive oil, butter, and even in some parts of the region, cream. The dish is eaten by dipping raw, boiled or roasted vegetables into the hot sauce and was viewed as good food for the cold weather, being eaten during the autumn and winter months, particularly at Christmas and New Year.

Once imported to Jersey, it moved out of Piedmontese homes to Jersey restaurants where it was frequently also seen on tables as a sauce served with certain foods, frequently as a dip with artichoke, and the name shifted linguistically to Bagna Calda.

Maybe that is a special case but, on the whole, changes came about at first slowly and often by chance, but then speeded up dramatically as the Italians settled down and put their own stamp on to their jobs. Bruno Zunino suggested that the Italian government should be eternally grateful to that generation of emigrants in the 1950s and 1960s: 'It was because of us that the huge export trade in foods and wines developed. It started to keep the Italian exiles happy and quite naturally people could see the possibilities of commercialising these products and so the market expanded.'

He said that he remembered the first *pasta faggioli* in London being listed on the menu in the Trattoria Toscana in Soho's Frith Street and at around the same time, *spaghetti vongole*, appeared there as did *vitello tonnato*. These traditional Italian regional dishes have become famous all over the catering world, having been seen and tried in London by the chattering classes and then quickly spread all over Britain via Italian restaurants in different communities, in cities across the country and then universally though the cook books.

Central London notwithstanding, the English as a race, at the time Giancarlo Mattioli arrived, were still very new to continental cooking and the presentation of food. And that is not surprising, given both the lack of foreign products as well as being in an Island cut off from Europe by the fortunes of war or just emerging from the era of austerity. And there was custom to overcome, for traditionally, there were certain things an Englishman would simply not do and eating garlic was one of them.

In his humorous recollections of life in a British Embassy in the Balkans after the war, Lawrence Durrell describes an exchange in which the Ambassador upbraids a junior attaché who he suspected of putting garlic in the food just served for an official lunch. 'Did you wittingly or unwittingly plug that cassoulet, impregnate that lustreless salad, order the peas to be lightly simmered in the stuff before serving? Answer me at once in Heaven's Name.'

Garlic was reserved for foreigners but, like it or not, it impregnated the new style of cooking and (just to confuse) other strange things appeared at the table. For example, what would a teenager being taken out to a good restaurant do when presented, for the first time ever, with an artichoke? How should it be approached? Giancarlo witnessed that type of culture shock on various occasions as new foods and strange implements provided fertile ground for confusion. Furthermore, the first impression of some dishes, as listed on a menu, was not guaranteed to appeal to a novice diner.

Snails and frog's legs were just not to be considered at first and took some time to get acceptance; new and strange-looking cold meats and salamis popped up. The stories abound: 'Well done steak tartar for example, but people learnt and they had to be helped and have matters explained tactfully by people like me. For them it was an education in new taste and new dishes.'

On the other hand, Giancarlo remembers him and his colleagues managing to make the best of things within the kitchens in which they worked: 'It wasn't easy, but we were lucky as we could create our own food. After all we were in the catering business; we knew what was in the food we wanted and so we would improvise.'

As he remembers, they ate on the job and so got given good basic food; it never crossed their minds at that time to go and get fish and chips for instance as, he maintains, it genuinely was not considered as their type of food. 'It would have been inappropriate for us, we thought.' Was it even good to taste? 'We didn't know and to be honest we didn't really want to know.

'Also, if we could find a shop that actually sold pasta - and nine times out of ten it was spaghetti and even then it was rare - we could cook our own food after service in the kitchen and make our own sauces. I come from near Bologna and, although our Bolognese sauce, as made in England, was nothing like the same as sauces from my home town, we improvised and made good food. Actually it wasn't always easy even to get decent mince meat to make the sauce and some of the English used to mix it with ketchup, and so we had to make do with that, as it was extremely difficult to find any tomato concentrate.'

Tino Rossi opened his Halkett Place restaurant La Capannina in 1966 and, by then, taste was changing. But it had taken time and so the notion that the Italians taught Jersey how to eat, while being an exaggeration, perhaps carries a grain of truth. According to Tino, he and his compatriots certainly did introduce certain unknown foods to the Island. There were some who used to say 'Italian cooking; that means spaghetti Bolognese'; after all, it had begun to appear in tins and was served at home on toast. There were also tins of 'alphabetti spaghetti', he recalled with just the hint of a shudder, but there were a growing number of potential customers who were more gastronomically aware.

'For example, simple extensions of the pasta range such as lasagne and cannelloni came as a surprise to many, but people started travelling and coming across more dishes when they were away, and then realised these could be found locally. After all, we, as a group, were happy to be able to show what Italian food could be.'

But the next stage came with designing the menu and finding special ingredients for the opening of La Capannina in 1966. How did he get the necessary Italian ingredients? Of course, having worked in Jersey at Hotel L'Horizon and the Star Restaurant in town as well as the Lobster Pot at L'Etacq, he was aware of what was missing and so he set out from day one to fill the gap. He used to buy, once a week from Covent Garden - 'a fantastic market in those days'- as there was no easy access in Jersey to European ingredients. 'I also used to buy through Genoa once a week; the air cargo or other transport charges were not too heavy back then so we could get produce over at a reasonable price. Obviously any truly Italian essentials came from there.'

The reality of course, behind these memories and the influences on local dining was that the Italians in the catering trade in Jersey were worked very hard; not that they expected anything else; it would have been the same wherever they might have settled. A local resident who knew Giancarlo when he arrived here to work said that there were occasions when he and his wife were doing multiple jobs during the winter to maximise their joint earnings: 'I had to, in order to survive in the winter; the wages in the catering business were not that big, so we had to take on extra regular, albeit occasional, employment, sometimes maybe two or three positions.

'That wasn't in the season of course; we didn't need to do that in the summer as we were working seven days a week and sometimes up to fifteen hours in any one day. The most we ever got in one week in the summer was about £31, but that was largely tips; the wage when I arrived was £4 - 4s (£4.20); the basic pay was pretty miserable.'

Angelo Mariani, as we have learnt, started in 1960 at the Hotel de France as a kitchen porter where he could work with his brother-in-law who was a 2nd chef; with luck, he could move up the ladder, get experience and improve his lot. Coming back the following year he had good news: 'The executive chef, Armando Nefroni, offered me a job as one of the breakfast chefs as well as doing a specific task, the middle course, for lunch and dinner. It was a step up, but I had to work for it. Imagine cooking breakfast for 450 staff and then 550 guests and starting at 6am in the morning.'

But it was a bit of a family-and-friends affair as his sister and a friend, were both on the coffee and tea; another colleague was doing the toast, another one the sausages. His brother-in-law had to fry over 2,000 eggs every morning: 'Just imagine four hours of frying eggs and no change in the task to keep your mind alive. And the chap who was just doing toast spent his time looking into two large salamander grills, going full-time, just to keep up with demand.'

Angelo was serving bacon directly from the hot trays to the waiters (about 95 of them) who were queuing up to take the plates and, at 6.30am, staff breakfast began. Angelo remembers there being 30 porters, 25 to 30 barmen, the builders, (there was always something going on) and the maintenance staff, then all the chambermaids and all the waiters: 'They all used to appear for breakfast and they were allowed exactly what they wanted, bacon, sausage, tomatoes, kippers, scrambled eggs, fried eggs. I lost a nail at least twice that year from the hot grease of the bacon and, after we had all eaten, the waiters would queue up again and the service for those staying at the hotel began and then I would serve the bacon for the guests, another 550 or so.'

He laughs now, but life as a junior chef in a large and busy hotel was never going to be easy. The activity for every minute of the day was, in effect, pre-ordained: 'I used to finish breakfast at about 10am, have a shower and a shave to freshen up, to be back by 11am and get ready for the middle course service at lunch. Everyone had to have the second course after the soup those days - it was the fish course - fish in breadcrumbs, fish in batter, and on Thursday it was always spaghetti.

'I remember a young Italo Miorin - later to be maître d'hôtel at the Pomme d'Or and for a long time president of the Jersey Branch of AMIRA (see chapter 10) - was one of the waiters.'

At midday Angelo and his colleagues sat down to eat whatever they were going to be served, and allowed for under the chef's percentage of food costs; there were 30 of the 'white jackets' who ate in a special room, then off they went to serve lunch and that would finish at about 3.30pm: 'After that, if the weather was nice, we would do a quick change, run all the way down St Saviour's Road, across Howard Davies Park on to the beach at the Dicq, ogle at the girls sun-bathing, have a swim, then run all the way back to be in the kitchen by five o'clock - what a rush.'

No eight hour days at that time, for the evening meal had to be prepared and, with luck, by 9 o'clock they had finished - unless, of course, there was a banquet that had to be prepared and served for 300 to 400 people. Then they had to clear down the kitchen and start from scratch setting it up for the next day; they would be there until 2am. 'For a banquet the head chef would get extra money but, for the rest of us, a crate of Mary Ann was brought in and we had a bottle of beer,' he remembers. 'For about four hours' extra work and they thought they were being generous! I remember my basic pay was £3 -10s a week. We got fed and a bed, which meant sharing a room with five others.'

But it was not only Angelo who worked those hours. He didn't mind that as such, but he would have preferred to work them for himself and not someone else, a course of action that eventually he followed - as did many others who saw a chance to make something for themselves in Jersey. And there were those like Angelo and others who we will meet soon, who met and married while in Jersey, which gave all of them an even greater incentive to succeed despite, in some cases, difficulties raised by the restrictions of the Bailiff's Permit.

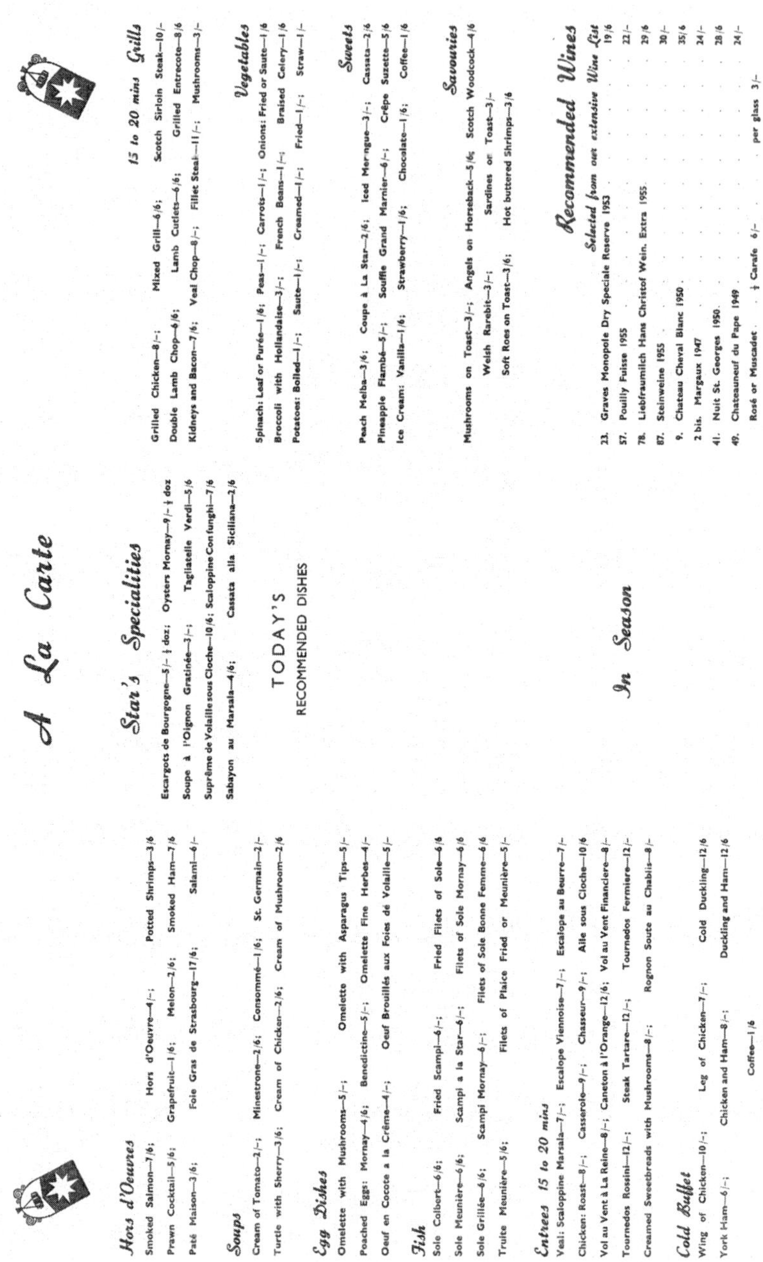

A La Carte

Hors d'Oeuvres
Smoked Salmon—7/6; Hors d'Oeuvre—4/-; Potted Shrimps—3/6
Prawn Cocktail—5/6; Grapefruit—1/6; Melon—2/6; Smoked Ham—7/6
Paté Maison—3/6; Foie Gras de Strasbourg—17/6; Salami—6/-

Soups
Cream of Tomato—2/-; Minestrone—2/6; Consommé—1/6; St. Germain—2/-
Turtle with Sherry—3/6; Cream of Chicken—2/6; Cream of Mushroom—2/6

Egg Dishes
Omelette with Mushrooms—5/-; Omelette with Asparagus Tips—5/-
Poached Eggs: Mornay—4/6; Benedictine—5/-; Omelette Fine Herbes—4/-
Oeuf en Cocote a la Crême—4/-; Oeuf Brouillés aux Foies de Volaille—5/-

Fish
Sole Colbert—6/6; Fried Scampi—6/-; Fried Filets of Sole—6/6
Sole Meunière—6/6; Scampi a la Star—6/-; Filets of Sole Mornay—6/6
Sole Grillée—6/6; Scampi Mornay—6/-; Filets of Sole Bonne Femme—6/6
Truite Meunière—5/6; Filets of Plaice Fried or Meunière—5/-

Entrees 15 to 20 mins
Veal: Scaloppine Marsala—7/-; Escalope Viennoise—7/-; Escalope au Beurre—7/-
Chicken: Roast—8/-; Casserole—9/-; Chasseur—9/-; Aile sous Cloche—10/6
Vol au Vent à La Reine—8/-; Caneton à l'Orange—12/6; Vol au Vent Financiere—8/-
Tournedos Rossini—12/-; Steak Tartare—12/-; Tournedos Fermiere—12/-
Creamed Sweetbreads with Mushrooms—8/-; Rognon Soute au Chablis—8/-

Cold Buffet
Wing of Chicken—10/-; Leg of Chicken—7/-; Cold Duckling—12/6
York Ham—6/-; Chicken and Ham—8/-; Duckling and Ham—12/6

Coffee—1/6

Star's Specialities
Escargots de Bourgogne—5/- ½ doz; Oysters Mornay—9/- ½ doz
Soupe à l'Oignon Gratinée—3/-; Tagliatelle Verdi—5/6
Suprême de Volaille sous Cloche—10/6; Scaloppine Con funghi—7/6
Sabayon au Marsala—4/6; Cassata alla Siciliana—2/6

TODAY'S
RECOMMENDED DISHES

In Season

15 to 20 mins Grills
Grilled Chicken—8/-; Mixed Grill—6/6; Scotch Sirloin Steak—10/-
Double Lamb Chop—6/6; Lamb Cutlets—6/6; Grilled Entrecote—8/6
Kidneys and Bacon—7/6; Veal Chop—8/-; Fillet Steak—11/-; Mushrooms—3/-

Vegetables
Spinach: Leaf or Purée—1/6; Peas—1/-; Carrots—1/-; Onions: Fried or Saute—1/6
Broccoli with Hollandaise—3/-; French Beans—1/-; Braised Celery—1/6
Potatoes: Boiled—1/-; Saute—1/-; Creamed—1/-; Fried—1/-; Straw—1/-

Sweets
Peach Melba—3/6; Coupe à La Star—2/6; Iced Meringue—3/-; Cassata—2/6
Pineapple Flambé—5/-; Souffle Grand Marnier—6/-; Crêpe Suzette—5/6
Ice Cream: Vanilla—1/6; Strawberry—1/6; Chocolate—1/6; Coffee—1/6

Savouries
Mushrooms on Toast—3/-; Angels on Horseback—5/6; Scotch Woodcock—4/6
Welsh Rarebit—3/-; Sardines on Toast—3/-
Soft Roes on Toast—3/6; Hot buttered Shrimps—3/6

Recommended Wines
Selected from our extensive Wine List

23.	Graves Monopole Dry Speciale Reserve 1953	19/6
57.	Pouilly Fuisse 1955	22/-
78.	Liebfraumilch Hans Christof Wein. Extra 1955	29/6
87.	Steinweine 1955	30/-
9.	Chateau Cheval Blanc 1950	35/6
2 bis.	Margaux 1947	24/-
41.	Nuit St. Georges 1950	28/6
49.	Chateauneuf du Pape 1949	24/-
	Rosé or Muscadet . ½ Carafe 6/-	per glass 3/-

The Star Menu from the late 50s – (1957/58).
Fashions change: The Liebfraumilch could command the same price as Nuits St Georges!

Chapter 4

STICKING TO IT

IT must have been very difficult to arrive in a strange land and start a new job, even if there were others from your country working alongside you to offer advice and help. Once the strangeness wore off there was the hard work - unremitting it seemed - with which to contend. But there was an aim in sight, whether it was learning a new language, acquiring new skills or making better money than was available back home, where jobs were few and far between.

But if the Italians who came here during this era had one thing in common, it was the drive to improve their lot so they could have a better life and, with luck, give their children (when and if they arrived) a better chance and thus a wider choice of careers.

The late Giuseppe Francescon came to Jersey in May 1966, later than some of those whom we have met. Many of his colleagues came over as part of a brigade, but not him. He decided to come over on his own. As he once said: 'On the way over I came across other people on their way to Jersey but I left my little village by myself to make my own way here. This was not the first time I had set off from home as, some years earlier, I had said goodbye and left to work in Germany.'

His memories, recorded for the BBC in his Halkett Place restaurant, Gio's, continued: 'It was part of a long-term plan, as my Father very wisely insisted I should learn not just a language, but languages. And so I went to Germany for three years, went to language school two or three times a week and, by the end of that time, I could speak pretty good German. Of course, to remain proficient in a language you have to speak it regularly and, as there aren't many Germans in Jersey on a regular basis, I now have a bit of a problem having a conversation with any customers from there, but it comes back when given a chance.'

But at the time Giuseppe came to Jersey (and also Maurizio Marzana who was another example of a late arrival), there was already a large Italian community and Jersey's catering industry was Italian. Or at least that was the popular perception as the Italians occupied very visible positions where they would interact with the customers. But whatever the actual number (and estimates vary), there were a lot of Italians in Jersey. But it was not to last for much longer.

'Yes, you're right. I don't know the numbers exactly but I was told in the early 1960s that there were many thousands of Italians over here. Maybe, maybe not, but it was certainly in the thousands. Nowadays, there are only a few hundred.'

Giuseppe remembered that when he arrived, the majority of the hotel staff was Italian, with a few Spanish and perhaps at that time some from Portugal and some Madeirans, as the next big influx was under way - and that was about it. Then at the end of the 1960s and in to the 1970s the change started to happen. 'People began to shift, maybe go to America like I did. I was there, on and off, for three years in America working from Miami on the cruise ships, but I always came back.'

He kept in touch with Jersey and that led to him staying here all his working life. 'The reason I returned was that the ship I was working on caught fire in the middle of the Gulf of Mexico. It was a Cunard ship, the *Cunard Ambassador* I think (and, before you ask, it was nothing to do with my flambé skills).'

He remembered being taken to Miami then, with many others, flown back to Europe and he was also given a ticket to join another ship, but he never made it. 'You see, when I got back to London I thought: "Why don't I pop down to Jersey for a bit and see my friends?" So I did,' he said, 'and I am still here. I never used that ticket as I met my wife on that visit and we married in 1976.'

But by then the UK had joined the Common Market and travel restrictions for European citizens had been reduced to virtually none. It had been different in earlier times as Giancarlo Mattioli remembered. As we have already heard, the Bailiff's permit specifically linked someone to the job, or at least the business sector for which he had originally applied to work. That meant, in effect leaving after six months, as a large proportion of the hotels were seasonal.

Breaking through that seasonal work barrier was the aim of many. As Giancarlo has already said, 'we had to stay here in guaranteed employment for eight years before we were free of that permit.' He says he managed to achieve that because he stuck to it and went out of his way to find winter employment, even if it meant working for many masters.

By the age of 27 or 28 Giancarlo had been here eight years. Having achieved that target, he was, as they used to say 'free of permit' and that released him from all controls. 'This meant I could rent or buy like a Jersey person or, and this was the path I took, start my own business. So I bought the lease of the Cafe Des Fleurs at 39, New Street, which we then renamed the Cafe Presto and, that was it. We were on our way and we never looked back.'

According to Giancarlo (and here he echoes Franco Gatti in a previous chapter), there were not many Jersey people at that time who wanted to work in the catering business. He said, according to friends who came to the Island in the early 1950s a few years before he arrived, the Italians very quickly became the principal group ensuring the brigades were properly set up and then run as they should be. They were sought after by the local hotel owners for they had the skills which were in demand.

Good chefs and waiters were poached from other hotels and any half decent catering worker who knew his job properly could soon easily find employment elsewhere. However, looking back and with hindsight, we can see that this reliance on a steady stream of immigrants, coupled with a desire to keep the good staff, would inevitably run into conflict with the strictures of the Bailiff's permit.

Thus it was that in 1961 when Angelo Mariani returned to Jersey for his second season, he found himself right in the middle of a major (and rather public) row. His family became involved in what was then viewed as, and what in retrospect could be confirmed as, the first dent in the Bailiff's permit rules and immigration system in Jersey.

Angelo had come to Jersey to join his brother-in-law, Guido Parmisani, who was married to Angelo's sister, Palmira Mariani. Guido worked as 2nd chef at the Hotel de France and Angelo was returning to take up a new role as a chef doing breakfast, as well as middle course for lunch and dinner. His sister and brother-in-law had a child, a baby girl called Anna who was born in December 1959. As a very young baby, Anna was looked after by her relations in Italy during the summer season of 1960. When Guido and Palmira returned for the new season in March 1961, they insisted that, unless they were allowed to bring their baby over to the Island, they would not stay.

This was when the head chef, Armando Nefroni, the manager of the hotel, John Howard, and the owners of the Hotel de France, Major Reynolds and Captain Reynolds, became involved. They did not want to lose Guido or Palmira, but the Aliens Office stated that they only had a permit to work, not a residential permit authorising them to settle in Jersey. Therefore, it would not be possible to allow Anna to be brought over. The value of having experienced staff to give continuity of service in the emerging and highly valued tourism sector was made crystal-clear to anyone who would listen. After a stand-off between the hotel and the Aliens Office, the civil servants blinked first and the Hotel de France won. The whole saga had, of course, been much to the interest of the rest of the hotel industry, who saw a precedent being created, and so the rules were adapted to allow for special circumstances.

Angelo remembers his sister, Palmira, taking Anna (by then 18 months old) every morning to a baby minder in Belmont Road and later the little girl achieved another first, being the first Italian-born girl to be educated at Beaulieu Convent School. Guido remained at the Hotel de France until 1970 when he, his wife, Palmira and brother-in-law, Angelo, bought Gimbels Restaurant in Colomberie, the first business in Angelo's long and successful Jersey career.

That was in 1961, but going back a few years to Giancarlo's early days, he like many others, wanted to stay in the Channel Islands - not least because of the fact he would have to go into the Army if he went back to Italy, but also because he saw opportunities here. However, the onus was on him to find employment in the winter - never an easy task with so many of his colleagues trying to do the same.

The first year he was in Jersey, he went on to Guernsey, then came back to Jersey and worked the season during the second year. He also brought his girlfriend, Antonietta, from Italy and married her at around this time. The wedding service was very much a do-it-yourself event. Earlier, he had gone back to his own town to look up Antonietta, who had grown up with him near Ferrara. They were school friends, 'kissing friends,' as Giancarlo put it, and he brought her over to Jersey and they quickly got married at St Thomas's Church in Val Plaisant.

He recalls that they only had a few guests, seven or eight perhaps, but he had to meet all the costs himself, including a nice white wedding dress and he remembers it as being a wonderful if, at times, slightly chaotic day. 'But there was one mistake. I forgot, or maybe I wasn't told, that, being a Catholic, I also had to marry in the registry office. Antonietta came into the church, the music started, and then the priest asked me for the certificate. "What certificate," I asked?

'The priest was wonderful. It was a good job it was a Saturday for he phoned down to the registry office on my behalf and managed, at the last moment, to get a registrar immediately. We went to his office, he arrived and did what was necessary there and then, and we got back into the taxi and returned to the church. It was just as well there were only a few guests otherwise it would have been a real shambles.'

He remembers he had to work all the previous night to prepare the reception, which was difficult. Being only 21, he didn't know about these things - back home all the arrangements would have been left to the parents. 'It was a nice display and it went well. We had taken over a room above West's Cinema which was normally used as the old dancing school. It was Brett's School of Dancing, a place I am sure many people of a certain age will remember.'

'By now, I was 21 and therefore allowed to work in England, so we both decided to give it a try for one winter. It was easy enough to get there but it was very different from Jersey, particularly the deductions they made from my wages before I saw any money.'

The other main problem facing Giancarlo, while working in London, was the cost of transport and the rent. He had to work as much as possible to make money, but even so, most of what he earned went on living. In London he worked in three places; he had to, otherwise it would have been subsistence-working with no added benefit to be had from savings. He discovered that he couldn't live anywhere near where he worked as that was right in the centre of the West End - that area was far too expensive for someone on his earnings to live. In order to find a decent yet affordable place to live, the answer was to go miles away, but the downside of that option was the long and expensive commute.

'We tried a compromise and found a place in King's Cross, which was not a nice area at all, but at least I could get to and from work on foot.'

As with many of his countrymen, Giancarlo was well aware that establishing the foundations for a genuinely better life in the future meant embracing the work ethic in the present. His time in London proved that. He would get up in the morning and set out to do two jobs on weekdays, both in the West End and City areas so he could get to them on foot. And then he did a different job on Sundays: 'At night I was in the Latin Quarter, a night club. That was from six in the evening until four or five in the morning. Then I would head back from the West End to Kings Cross in the early-hours, have a rest, but only a brief one, as I had to get to work in the City by 11 o'clock. By half past I had set up for the lunch, and that was a four-hour shift.' That gave him two hours to have a brief rest, change and head back to The Latin Quarter.

Sunday was a free day, in theory, but that was an opportunity to earn a bit more, so he signed on to serve the large parties at the Mecca Function Rooms in Tottenham Court Road, only quite a short walk from his room in King's Cross: 'I was lucky to find that as an extra job and my wife, Antonietta, worked there with me as well, as a waitress.' He recalls it being quite well paid for the time, receiving a basic £5 for a day's work - a full day at that, for they would start at nine in the morning and work through until ten or eleven at night.

He would be given a table of 12 to 14 people as his station and they would be eating all day, or so it seemed to his tired feet: 'I had never seen so much food disappear!' Furthermore, making sure of that all-important tip to make the day worthwhile, was hard work in itself. In the end he would have to go round the tables dropping heavy hints: 'Have you had a nice meal? Was everything to your satisfaction and was the service satisfactory?'

'Sometimes I would then get a slightly grudging half-a-crown, or two shillings or, as I learnt to call it, a two-bob-bit. But half-a-crown was good money back then; it would be the equivalent of getting five pounds today.'

Franco Gatti points out how different were the customs and assumptions about what a boss could expect from the staff. 'You must remember that in those days there was absolutely no protection for the waiter. You worked 12 hours a day, often even longer, and you did it or you were out and if you lost your job and did not have a reference you were back in Italy. You could never run a business like that nowadays. But I would guess that in Italy the situation was probably worse. That's the way things were.'

Franco worked at The Olwyn Grove and the hotel also housed the first incarnation of the Tropicana, which he guessed was perhaps the only singing and dancing 'night club' in Jersey in those days. 'It was full of young men and young women enjoying each other's company.' And he also said that, no matter how bad the hours, you could have some social life, for it was easier in Jersey than in Italy, where the management was on your back all the time. 'Jersey was better in that respect without any doubt. You could at least have a life.'

Angelo Mariani has already made mention of Italo Miorin, who features later in this book. Italo started his career in Jersey working as a waiter in the dining room of the Hotel de France in 1961; by 1970 Italo had become the maître d'hôtel at the Pomme d'Or, where he was Angelo Saccone's first boss. Angelo, as we have learnt, had arrived in Jersey from Palermo with, in effect, a brief stop at Lido de Jesolo, and an even briefer stop in the Isle of Man where, soon after his arrival, the hotel at which he was employed went under. By then, Italo had developed into an impressive 'old school' maître, proud of his training and the tradition of his chosen profession. This was a man who always insisted on work in his (note 'his' and not 'the Seymour Family's' or 'the Pomme d'Or's') dining room, being completed correctly and with no short cuts. He was a stickler for training and proper presentation and service.

We will meet him later as the first Fiduciario (president) of AMIRA *(Associazione Maîtres D'hôtel Italiani Ristoranti e Alberghi)* - the association of Italian maîtres in restaurants and hotels in Jersey. In that capacity he organised many of their tremendously enjoyable and high profile 'eno-gastronomic' evenings. There, over the years, many hundreds of people would marvel at their skills and then sample the taste of what could be produced with lamp cooking by Jersey's top maîtres. And he insisted on the same standards in the Pomme d'Or dining room. The story is told of one occasion when he was inspecting what to most people's perception was a beautifully laid table for a big dinner; he saw some of the cutlery was slightly sticking out over the edge. He ran his hand down the side of table, scattering the cutlery and disrupting the whole lay out, before ordering the staff to do it again, and this time properly.

Strict and old school indeed, but that was the point. For Italo, like any good maître, was a perfect conduit for passing on knowledge, practice and tradition.

As Angelo Saccone recalls, 'working for someone like Italo, you had to be aware of everything, even your posture and the way you walked. But I tell you, looking back, I don't regret one bit of it because of what I learned. He taught me everything - technique, recipes for the lamp and how to deal with strange situations that might arise. A young man could not have had a better role model as a tutor.'

When Angelo started at the Pomme d'Or he was the lowest of the low, a *commis débarasseur,* whose traditional duties would include ensuring that all dirty items were removed to be washed up and to ensure that the sideboard was left clear and well stocked. He would also be responsible for the cleaning of the dining room during the preparation for service.

'We really had to work hard,' Angelo remembers. 'There were regular events throughout the day to occupy your time: breakfast, mid-morning coffee, afternoon tea and dinner. Obviously, this was split into different shifts, but the week had to be covered so it was a seven-day-a-week schedule for which I received £13.50 plus my share of the tronc (pooled tips). As a junior commis, I always reckoned I did the hardest work and got the least reward because of the point system. But it got better - I was a chef de rang by the end of my time there and was breakfast head waiter.'

Angelo was lucky to get a job at the Pomme d'Or because it was one of the hotels that remained open all year. During the winter it was very well used by a regular clientele of commercial travellers coming over to 'do Jersey' and although the number of staff was reduced, it was not by very much. And, of course, there were the Christmas and New Year celebrations which kept everyone busy: 'I remember one New Year's Eve, I got into an argument with Italo (I was wrong but wouldn't admit it) and Italo - quite rightly in retrospect - sacked me. Luckily, Piero Alonghi, the other head waiter who worked in another part of the hotel, immediately took me on (don't worry about it, he said, he got rid of you, now you come and work with me) and the situation quickly resolved itself.'

Five years at the Pomme d'Or and in 1975 Angelo married Rosemary, a girl from Wincanton in Somerset, whom he had met locally and, settling down, he decided that he wanted to spend evenings at home with her. Apart from that, she didn't like the idea of him working late every night: 'She was the window dresser at British Home Stores and I met her at Lord's discotheque.' It was time for him to leave the catering business.

The significance of that summary of Angelo leaving the catering business is its importance to one overriding aspect of the story of the Italians who arrived during this period and who decided to stay. It is the story of integration into the local community and the ability, while not losing sight of their Italian background, heritage, and love of Italian products (not least Alfa Romeo cars), they still managed to avoid the temptation of emulating the American pioneers in the western movies - driving the wagons into a circle and firing out at the local inhabitants.

They might have stuck, for many years, to what they knew best and (as many have remembered) the waiters might often go to the back of the kitchen and make a meal out of what they could find, or had maybe been left out for them by a sympathetic chef. And it wasn't just quick snacks, for they were cooking their own flambés or steak in some special sauce cooked in the pan; after all they were professionals. But clinging on to their background in this and in other ways did not prevent them, at the same time, from blending into society.

At the end of his first season at the Hotel de l'Europe, Mauro Mori left the Island to take up a job in Holland but that was a very unhappy time as there were only three Italians there and the rest of the waiting and kitchen staff were German and Dutch and they fought (literally) the whole time. 'The idea was to go for six months but I could only stand it for three,' he said. He remembers there being three or four fights, at least, every day: 'It was a dreadful atmosphere to work as you were walking on eggshells the whole time.

'They wanted me to stay on and offered me a three-year contract, but I thought: "No, I am going back to Jersey. I have already been offered a job as a head waiter (at L'Europe) and have a lovely lady waiting for me." I had fallen in love with Irene. She was a wonderful person. I met her in the first year as she was doing everything, manageress, head housekeeper, head barman, head receptionist. She did the bloody lot.'

It was the right decision. Mauro and Irene became a long standing and devoted couple and, during their time together, created the perfect atmosphere and working arrangement that made Mauro's Restaurant in La Motte Street the success it was.

As Bruno Zunino commented, 'I remember at the end of the 1950s into the 1960s there were about 2,500 to 3,000 Italians here in Jersey. However, later, when things got better in Italy, many of them went back. Several hundred (I don't know how many) stayed in Jersey. They settled, married English girls, started their own businesses, brought up their children and that makes up the majority of those who are still here. The Italian community in Jersey has remained like one large family. But even so there is no sense now, nor was there really back then, of there being a community within a community with strict dividing lines. We integrated well with the local population, the larger community.'

Indeed they did. Those who did well became accepted members of the business community, not as Italian businessmen, but as businessmen who happened to be Italian - and there is a world of difference between those two descriptions.

Much has been made of the training and skill of those who came to Jersey during the 20 years or so of the major Italian influx. And those who came brought with them, not only the skills which added a sense of theatre to dining out, but also the discipline and teamwork of the brigade. It was this that helped them, not only to settle in by starting out in familiar surroundings in a strange country, but eventually that also gave many of them confidence to take their skills out of the large dining rooms and into their own businesses. This was ultimately for the benefit of local residents as much, if not more, than the tourists, and the background experience of the brigade system was crucial in giving the catering industry in Jersey a great legacy.

Chapter 5

THE BRIGADIERS

A RECURRENT theme emerging from the memories of the Italians who arrived in Jersey during the 1960s is that many of them say that they joined a brigade, rather than becoming a member of staff at a hotel. For example, Tino Rossi, as we read earlier, described his coming to Jersey back in the early 1950s thus: 'In my case, the permit was issued by the Hotel L'Horizon who made all the arrangements. However, in my mind I was employed, not so much by the hotel, but the brigade that was then run by Giuseppe Panigarda.'

It may be difficult to imagine but there was a time when the world of commerce wasn't ruled by human resource managers with their own particular processes of recruitment and staff management. Many of the Italians came to Jersey in large numbers after the war were recruited by men who actually understood the job, could do it themselves, and whose reputations were built on arriving with a fully qualified and cohesive team around them. It sounds revolutionary, even today. And many who were in the tourism industry at the time say - when looking back - that the huge benefit of the Italian influx of the 1950s was that they had the training ethic. It was not a case of: 'I'll be a waiter for a time; it doesn't look too difficult.'

The simple ingredient and also the driver of Italian success in the acclaimed hotels and dining rooms of that era was the strength of the brigade system, which ensured that staff arrived trained at least to the level for which they were required. If a young man wanted to attain a high position within the catering hierarchy, get a close look at, and cater to, those with a lifestyle that he could normally only marvel at in magazines, there was a way open for him. More importantly, if he wished to gain marketable skills, then, during this era, one of the proven ways of achieving all this was to join a brigade; in effect become a 'brigadier'.

Jersey hoteliers, therefore, could rely on brigades arriving with skilled staff to run their dining rooms (and kitchens) efficiently from day one and then, when necessary, to keep it topped up with the right talent. It was not just the number of Italians who arrived in Jersey that made the impression on the local catering and hospitality industry - it was the skills they brought with them.

As Tino Rossi remembers: 'The Italians arrived here in big numbers during the 1950s and 1960s. And, as I have said before, we would be employed by the maître d'hôtel who would create and run that brigade. Also, there were some maîtres who would take a whole brigade over to Jersey for the season. Of course, in those days the season used to be from March (you remember the honeymooners?) and would tend to go through, for some, at least, until the end of October. With the hotels closed we would have to find somewhere else to go for the winter season.'

In effect, therefore, the specialist work in the dining room and kitchen was sub-contracted. All the hassle of employing staff was taken away from the hotelier for whom the prime, perhaps the only, concern in relation to those departments was to find a good maître d'hôtel or chef he could trust to produce the goods and so build up a mutually beneficial and long term relationship.

And this isn't a nostalgic, sepia tinted view; it happened often. John Wileman, for example, who took over as manager of Hotel L'Horizon in 1966, remembers going into the dining room on the first weekend he was there: 'On my first Sunday, I wept! The buffet lunch was exquisite in its preparation and layout - I had never seen anything like it (well, not since Westminster Hotel School, ten years earlier). The same applied to the silver service in the restaurant; everything was a prideful joy and just as it should be. Mainly responsible was the Italian hotel staff, in particular, Piero Alzetta (the head chef) and Aldo Valli (the restaurant manager).'

This was a pleasant experience for John, but in one sense it was not a surprise so much as a reaffirmation of what he already knew: 'I'd spent some time in 1958 as a trainee at Rome's Hotel Excelsior on the Via Veneto so I knew how special the Italians were at all things connected with catering.'

It was a time when being a waiter was very different. Today, at its most basic, a waiter picks up a plate from the kitchen-pass and, with a suitably sepulchral expression, takes it to the table to present with whatever flourishes the establishment allows. Back in the period we are examining, there were a whole range of activities in the dining room and a whole range of skills, all part of the brigade system that was itself built around a genuine promotional ladder.

In essence, the brigade was a highly structured hierarchy based on a combination of skill, training and experience. The commis waiter was the lowest-ranked waiter in a restaurant, the entry level for a young man fresh out of catering school in Italy. Sometimes a college would partner with, or indeed own, a hotel so that promising youngsters like a young Maurizio Marzana could learn while actually perfecting the job they were hoping to fill.

And if ever the point was to be made about young men coming to Jersey fully trained, this was it. Maurizio came to Jersey with experience in some well known and very good hotels in Germany and Switzerland but, before those times he went to catering school at a beach resort near Rome. The Hotel Castelfusano was set in a park by the beach, an area set aside by the authorities for leisure that also included a country club and a campsite. The hotel itself was actually run by ENALC (the Catering College) so you could get work experience, train and study in one place. According to Maurizio, there was, at the time, professional and award-winning staff in every department. For example, the head waiter who ruled the dining room was a grand maître della ristorazione and the barman had won many a national competition. The students learnt every aspect of the hotel trade from masters of their craft. They were divided into two brigades and half the time you studied and the other half you worked in the hotel in all the different positions.

But, however well trained a young man such as Maurizio might have been, he would always start at the bottom as a commis, a term which covers a multitude of activities. Some restaurants use the terms 'commis de rang' and 'commis waiter' interchangeably, but in the traditional brigade system, commis de rang is one of three types of commis waiter who help with food and drink service. The other two are the commis de suite who carries the food from the kitchen to the dining room and the commis de débarrasseur who collects the dirty plates and serving dishes from the gueridon and takes them back to the kitchen. Whether there was a complete multi-layered brigade system depended on the size of the restaurant, the complexity of its operations and, of course, the type of customer who patronised the restaurant or hotel dining room.

And there was another aspect of learning the job that was important. All those Italians who came to Jersey during this time arrived with the express wish to learn English and so give themselves a better chance to improve their prospects. No matter, therefore, how good you were, or thought you were, when you arrived in Jersey, language was a vital part of your portfolio of marketable skills.

Eric Ruaro came to Jersey after a spell in a ski resort in the Dolomites and was well qualified. He applied to Aldo Valli at Hotel L'Horizon and there he was, but at a very basic level. At the Hotel L'Horizon, at that time, there were ten stations and as a commis he was entitled to one day off in ten. His basic wages were £4/16/4 (£4.82) and with tips he could, at the start of his time there, bring it up to around £6 per week. As Eric saw it he was pretty lucky, not well paid but it was a job, it was clean and he was well fed.

'And don't forget,' he said, 'at that time if you didn't speak English, you couldn't get near a customer. Your job was to get the food from the kitchen and bring it to the gueridon where the chef de rang would take over. You would get promoted if and when your language was good enough to have a sensible conversation with the customer and in my view that was absolutely correct.'

It would be no exaggeration to say that the Italians, who were a vital part of the catering trade in Jersey at the time, had professionalism drilled into them from an early age - not only through training and experience but also because of expectation from the existing culture. Looking back and listening to the comments of those who were there at the time, it could be summarised that it was a case of 'get trained and do the job properly' rather than 'do the job and get paid'. Maybe that is a bit simplistic, but Eric, when comparing then to now, is surprised at the level of skills now deemed acceptable.

'I'm from the old school and it was quite simple; if you didn't know your job you either wouldn't get employed or you started at the bottom and learnt it. If you tried to bluff it, you wouldn't last five minutes.'

And the late Giuseppe Francescon came through the same mill. Once he came to Jersey, and despite his proven skills, he had to start again as a commis waiter because he couldn't speak English: 'Then when my language improved I was quickly promoted to match my qualifications, as chef de rang, being in charge of say half a dozen tables.' Beyond that someone could specialise and become a sommelier or choose to head for management and become assistant maître d'hôtel. But right from the start qualifications were essential, otherwise no one would employ you to do a proper job with prospects.

Eric Ruaro put the same thing a little more bluntly: 'Yes - and it is this level of skill and qualification that is lacking now. If you were not properly trained back then, you washed the dishes. End of story.'

Giuseppe scaled that ladder and became the head of the dining room at Hotel L'Horizon, and indeed 'Head Waiter of the Year 1989' for the whole United Kingdom. It all seems a bit different, in as much as being a waiter seemed to be more of a profession at that time, carrying with it recognised and genuine levels of achievement.

'Yes, of course it was more of a profession,' he continued. 'Now, everything is changed and food is all plated, whereas before you came to the table and you served the customer from the gueridon or you prepared a flambé in front of the customer. Style and a sense of theatre really mattered; it is not the same anymore.'

Some of the skills required seemed a bit archaic, but that is what was required. Eric mentioned bringing food to the gueridon; Giuseppe talked of serving food from the gueridon. That was the trolley or sometimes fixed serving station where the good chef de rang or one of his senior assistants really came to the fore. Gueridon service is largely a thing of the past, the young commis waiters were not allowed anywhere near a customer; the commis de suite, the one who goes to the kitchen and comes back with all the food, brought it to the gueridon and from then on the other people took charge.

The food being served was partially or mostly prepared in the kitchen then the experienced dining room staff would do the final assembly or cooking on the trolley at the side of the restaurant or, if there was room, by the customer's table. This might involve a flambé, or carving a joint, portioning a bird, or tossing a salad, filleting a fish and then rebuilding it without the bones, whatever was required. The serving station was equipped with a burner for cooking that could have been powered by gas, or spirits. This could be used for a flambé obviously, but most of the time it was to ensure that the food, when served, was hot.

Some gueridon stations might have had a cold drawer as well. All would have been equipped with a chopping board and cutlery drawer and have been supplied with the necessary utensils to prepare and serve whatever food the restaurant offered.

Looking across a busy dining room, it could be seen that the activity centred around the gueridon would have been repeated across the dining room as each station of between five to ten tables would have been similarly equipped. It was very organised and structured.

And with gueridon service, of course, an essential part of the job was making sure the food was served hot, nothing tiede, as can now be advertised on menus, which some say is there to compensate for the delay caused by serving and plating up. After his time at L'Horizon, Giuseppe would hark back to the skills which were required and, of course, that part of the job that was keeping food hot: 'All that is old world now and I'm sorry to see it go. It makes me a bit sad.' The idea of serving something lukewarm by design was something he could not accept.

On leaving catering school, Maurizio's first job was to be attached to a brigade in the Grand Hotel Regina in Grindelwald, a village in Switzerland's Bernese Alps, a popular gateway for the Jungfrau area, with skiing in winter and hiking in summer, or for the less active, catching the train up the Jungfrau.

According to Maurizio, it was viewed as one of the top tier of hotels in the whole of Europe and the guests reflected that, as at all the hotels in which he worked at this stage of his career.

In the Bellevue Palace in Berne, for example, beautifully located overlooking the river, large parties hosted by Embassies were a common feature: 'Huge banquets with up to 1,500 people sitting down - something I had never seen, nor have many others, I expect.'

He described how it would take about 12 staff simply to place a table cloth that was 50 metres long which, once on the table, was then ironed again. Then there was the laying up that would take about four hours: 'Everything perfectly aligned, with four or five glasses. You really don't see that sort of attention to detail any longer and, what's more, the amount of staff required to give such service is another aspect of the trade that has passed into memory. There is nowhere now that can afford to employ that many staff and give that sort of service.'

With a background in a brigade (that, of course, provided an opportunity to observe, and learn from, the skills and technique of the more experienced colleagues), everyone benefitted. Furthermore, that generation of Jersey hoteliers had an assurance that, whether they were signing up a brigade or an individual, they were also hiring experience and recognised qualifications so one problem, at least, was removed from their in-tray.

Beyond the role of commis would be a demi (assistant) chef de rang and eventually the chef de rang. He was the waiter in charge of a station in a restaurant, which could be up to ten tables. Customer service was the prime focus of the role. Excellent organisational skills would be required, as what was needed was a smooth flow of food coming out from the kitchen at the right time for each of the tables. In that way the team of waiters could move seamlessly from table to table with no sense of hurry; certainly never any hint of panic.

The chef de rang would in effect be the one who controlled the immediate experience of the diner, from table layout to knowledge of what was on offer, how it was prepared, then presenting the food, all combined to encourage the customer to return. Couple that with being impeccably dressed for the role, staying calm, and having a talent for running a well-trained team and it soon becomes clear that a good chef de rang was worth his weight in gold.

Giancarlo Mattioli came to Jersey in the 1950s when, he said, a waiter was viewed as a professional for many reasons: 'Not only in serving food, but being able to prepare and cook it as well. There were other strange but necessary skills such as being able to peel a grape with a fork and a knife. It's not easy, believe you me, but it can be done and we did it because that is what we were trained to do in Italy in the big hotels during the season.'

Maurizio Marzana recalls his background and early career from and how, when arriving in Jersey, he also chose to slip back down the ladder at the Hotel L'Horizon until his English improved. He said that in Germany he was seen as a good chef de rang with his own station. This would mean having a supporting staff to serve the eight tables in the station from his gueridon thus keeping the commis débarasseur very busy. The latter, as he reminds us, was the young man whose sole job was, during meal times, to carry all the dirty serving dishes, plates and cloches from the gueridon to the kitchen and, in some places, fetch the cooked food back for the next service. Maurizio's previous hotel had been on the Baltic coast in Germany, the 'Maritim' at Timmendorfer Strand, which had 20 stations in a huge restaurant about 100 metres long overlooking the beach.

'And all the guests wanted their food served hot on hot plates with all the final preparations being made at the table. The total opposite from now, but we had the manpower to do it.'

Diners at that time, especially younger diners approaching adulthood, saw the final gueridon preparation as an essential part of eating out. It was a sense of theatre, something special being laid on just for them. Dining out was more than eating; it was a demonstration of how things should be done.

Maurizio remembers: 'That was the sort of thing we would learn at catering school. Debone any fish, how to carve a duck or serve a chateaubriand, and of course you had to sharpen knives without cutting yourself or wounding the clients!'

He said that, for example, if a guest fancied an orange you didn't just put the orange on a plate and put it in on the table. As a chef de rang, he had his own little sharp knife. With this he skinned and cleaned the orange in front of the customers, segment it if necessary without cutting the inner skin and display the whole thing as a flower or whatever took your fancy: 'Perhaps you might squeeze a little orange juice onto the segments, add a little spirit or desert wine and serve it to the customer. Of course it all took time but that didn't matter, it had to look and taste good. It gave me satisfaction to see the finished work and note the customer's approval. Apart from anything else, it's a nice way of eating an orange.'

Anyone who has tried at home to emulate the way an experienced waiter can serve a mango will know what he is talking about. It all takes training and lots of practice, or as Maurizio said rather self-deprecatingly: 'If you know what to do it's easy to do it.'

One of the latest arrivals in this group of Italians who came to Jersey during the two decades of high immigration was Paulo Crolla, who was only just over 17 when he arrived at the Hotel de Normandie in Havre des Pas. The permit still existed, but with more hotels and restaurants staying open all year round to provide for a Jersey population which was increasingly enjoying the experience of dining out, it was easier to stay. As Paulo said, if you managed to find another job in the catering industry the Aliens Office would - and he was not quite sure on this point - either extend it or issue a new one. Anyway, someone could stay on as long as he had employment.

'I was lucky, I stayed. I came over when I was 17 ½ and by the end of the season I thought to myself there was no point in going back. Luckily the head of my brigade knew someone at the Little Grove Hotel - then a very smart place and what would now be called a 'boutique hotel' (it had not become a nursing home) - who needed some staff. So the man who brought me over to Jersey had a word with the head waiter at the Little Grove; he gave me a good reference and so I got a job there and stayed for a couple of years.'

Paulo's story provides an interesting example of the working of the brigade system with head waiters arranging transfers between themselves. The comparison of maîtres to the managers of sports teams becomes more understandable. The brigade was endemic in the culture and it was up to the individual members to try and get employed in the one of their choosing.

Paulo, and others such as Maurizio, were well aware of the necessity for making the best choice, for if someone was lucky to be in the right place where the head waiter was obviously a strong and successful person, an ambitious young man could stand out because of the quality of his work - and that could prove to be fortunate. The maître might be choosing a new team and being a member of it could then deliver guaranteed employment and therefore wages in the next place, wherever that might prove to be.

'A lot of guys I knew would stay with a particular maître and go, literally, all over the world,' said Paulo. 'If you are in a successful team with a good manager, why move unless you really want to stay in a particular place? So many stayed with a brigade because they trusted the maître, knew him as a man who knew what he wanted and what had to be done to deliver the result well and efficiently. It was a pleasure for us to be part of the brigade because you had such good experience working with the senior guys who, put together, had such a history of knowledge and experience.'

To a young man, therefore, a good brigade was employer, teacher and counsellor. The combined knowledge of those working would be immense and whatever question a junior might have about food or service the answer was there, either delivered privately or in a more formal setting, as Paulo remembers.

'I always remember those days when, before the start of any service, we all used to line up, like an army inspection parade, where we were told about the day's specials, how they were made what was in them, and we obviously had to make a point of remembering, even if it meant taking notes to look at later, in case the customers were to ask. The response

"I had better go and check it out" you get nowadays would simply not have been acceptable. If we didn't know we would have been in serious trouble.'

Victor Cornaglia stayed one season at Bouley Bay and then left in the winter to work in London where he got a job as head waiter at the Hotel Normandie in Knightsbridge. Once there he had no plans to return to Jersey. But that was soon to change as the owners of the Water's Edge Hotel found out where he was, rang to inform him they had parted company with their head waiter and would he please come back to Jersey and set up his own brigade at their hotel. He accepted and was there for nearly eight years through to 1962.

He looks back on those times very nostalgically. 'It was a lovely hotel with some very rich regulars and the scale of tipping was enormous. I had one tip for £75 which enabled me to buy a car and from others I would get £50 for the staff and a further £50 for me, even £100 was not unknown. In real terms these days, that was an enormous amount and, compared to today, was at a much greater scale.'

Paulo Crolla was telling us of the waiters lining up to be informed of the menu and the dish of the day perhaps, but equally important, if you were a senior waiter, was being aware of what the chef had bought in as a one off for the speciality of the day and what, therefore, was needed to be sold. The importance of this is illustrated by a story from Victor Cornaglia.

After several years at the Bouley Bay Hotel, Victor went to London and applied for a job as a head waiter at the Savoy Hotel. He was told they needed a head waiter for one of the dining rooms but they would not engage him until they had seen him work and could prove he had the skill and the experience. It was nothing personal, but a standard procedure for any potential employees of that rank.

'So, I looked around and found they worked basically the same system as the Normandie in Knightsbridge. Then a stroke of luck, for I bumped into Silvino Trompetto, who in 1962 had been made maître de cuisine, the first London-born man to reach that pinnacle.

Victor said he asked him for any tips or suggestions, 'and Trompetto said, "I have six ducks just arrived and I will put them aside for your restaurant, the River Room. If you can sell them I will back you for the job." So, that evening, I quickly sold the six ducks and then went back into the kitchen to ask if he had any more. 'After that I became Trompetto's friend for life.'

Victor Cornaglia, Italo Miorin, (centre) with catering royalty, (far left) Silvino Trompetto Maitre de Cuisine Savoy Hotel and (far right) Luigi Zambon Restaurant Manager Savoy Hotel. At the AMIRA Jersey stand at the Italian Trade Centre, Piccadilly, London 1984

Ida Rossi, of La Capannina at the Italian Food Fair

AMIRA Evening - Piero Guglieri and Giuseppe Francescon with zabaglione

AMIRA out in force

Visiting Amirini with (left) Maurizio Marzana, (4th from left) Carlo Ragazzi and (2nd from right) Paulo Crolla

Setti Pozzi, Mirto Sappé and Renzo Martin,
A long way, and many years, from the Turin Palace

Italo Miorin left with Hamish Marett-Crosby at AMIRA stand at the Italian Trade Centre, Piccadilly, London 1984

Franco Morosino and Elio Icardi

Renzo Martin, Setti Pozzi and Mirto Sappé,
A grand total of around 150 years in Jersey

Eric Ruaro, when Director of Merchant Vintners
showing how it's done

Setti Pozzi in front of The Apple Cottage (with a very large and rather surprised bass)

Italo Miorin, long time Fiduciario (president) of AMIRA Jersey

Paulo Crolla - Still working

Commendatore Luigi Forte

Miss Battle being presented with one of her prizes by Eric Ruaro

Eric Ruaro - "open air corkscrew king"

Paulo and his team at the Mary Rose Restaurant in Bath Street. Note, Paulo's Apron "Not only am I perfect, I'm Italian too

Victor went on to say that every time Silvino produced something a bit special, something a bit different, he would come to me to say: 'You are the only one who can sell anything I particularly want to go.'

Victor would stay in the River Room until 1966 and he was not the only man to admire the chef's work. He told a story how the general manager one night asked Sir Winston Churchill what he had thought of the dinner prepared with greatest care by Silvino Trompetto. Sir Winston didn't reply immediately. The manager thought there was something very wrong. After a while, the great statesman sighed and said: 'When I die, and if I have a choice, I'd rather have The Savoy staff looking after me in Heaven instead of angels.'

For the older men of this generation of Italians, training and getting experience in the brigade had a further difficulty in that the international language of catering, menu writing, as well as food preparation and cooking was French.

Tino Rossi remembers: 'In my training as an aspiring commis waiter who wanted to rise in my chosen profession, I was taught the classical way; the French way. Oh yes, French was the language of haute cuisine even in Italy. I would go to the kitchen as a commis waiter to collect a dish and if I didn't give it its proper name in French I would be sent back to the maître d'hôtel to ask him how to say it in French. It was like being called up before the head master in school, I soon learnt. Believe it or not, everything had to be in French, even in Italy.

'But of course that created problems for the new class of diners anxious to go out and join in; keen to become a part of this new fashion of eating out more. They were expected to know, for example, the difference between *sole dieppoise* and *sole véronique*. Not knowing could create problems for a *dieppoise* sauce contains small prawns, or shrimps, whereas a *véronique* uses grapes; it could be very dangerous for any diner with a shellfish allergy to order the wrong one by mistake. Not everyone knew, of course, and they relied on the senior waiting staff, very diplomatically and delicately, to guide them'.

He continued: 'On modern menus now you get a lot of explanations and details about the dish, almost to the extent of giving the recipe in some places. Back then it had a name, bestowed on it by one of the famous chef/founders of haute cuisine, and it was part of the repertoire. The sophisticated client was supposed to know exactly what it was.

'Looking back, those who seemed to remember most about these details were the wives and often I have heard, for example, a local business leader or member of the high society, turn to his wife to remind him how the sole *bonne femme*, for example, was made.'

So the young men learning the social skills of dining out had to learn what to order and, when it arrived, how to eat it. Some of Jersey Italian community would tell stories of passing a table and hearing the crunch, crunch of a snail shell being opened up, if not chewed, to discover the contents. Then there was the horror of first being presented with an artichoke with no instructions as to how to approach it. You relied on the head waiter to explain, tactfully and politely.

'Yes indeed. Artichokes were always a problem for the newcomer,' said Tino, and even asparagus would confuse some people who would eat the base and leave the tip. Tact was required because no one wants to feel small in front of a table companion who they are trying to impress.'

The brigades instructed their members in the more esoteric food and recipes as well the social mores of the dining room. The brigadiers had connections to, or experience of, some of the most notable establishments in Europe. They then guided, perhaps even taught, the diners. When bringing in and making use of that experience, many made Jersey their home and, in so doing, opened the door to a more international cuisine and way of dining, which speeded up the change in Jersey's catering industry - much to the benefit of the Island's tourism sector.

John Wileman, the manager of the Hotel L'Horizon in 1966 through to the mid 1980s, summed up what to him was the importance of this group of professionals: 'The Italians of the 1960s and 1970s formed the bedrock of the fine Island cuisine of today. I used to say that, in my day, an Island visitor could, during a fortnight's visit to Jersey, wine and dine in the finest of restaurants each day of their stay.'

Chapter 6

PROFESSIONALISM

THE arrival of the Italians had a huge impact on the Jersey catering industry. John Wileman, the manager of the Hotel L'Horizon during the period of the Italians arriving - and then becoming, in his view, the face of Jersey dining - put it very strongly. He said they created the bedrock on which Jersey's reputation as a fine dining destination was founded.

There are those who remember the 1950s and early 1960s in Jersey very clearly who say the Italians taught Jersey how to eat - a pardonable exaggeration perhaps?

A view from inside the industry at this time can be provided by the Seymour family, the driving force of Seymour Hotels - now in the third generation of family control since the war. The estate during this period included the Pomme d'Or, The Portelet, The Merton, the Hotel de la Plage and La Coie. The latter, or at least its site, is now given over to States housing and a glance at the size of that development gives a clue as to how big La Coie Hotel actually was: 'The largest guest house in the Channel Islands,' according to Robin Seymour.

He considers that the Italians brought to the Island the type of catering and the type of service that many Islanders of the class who had travelled abroad were used to receiving at top hotels in Germany, Switzerland and in Italy, or, for example, Reid's Hotel in Madeira.

'Their arrival brought Jersey into that type of hospitability and service. So to say they taught Jersey how to eat was right to an extent but I assume those who said so had travelled, and travelled well.'

However, Robin stressed that this Italianisation of the catering industry could not apply to the whole of the Island at that time as there was a wide range of customers coming to Jersey who all wanted something which suited them; not everyone thought the same way. 'Tourism was a multi-layered beast, but yes, the Italians certainly had an influence on those upper, and perhaps more visible, layers.'

He also reckons that they also imported - again, to a degree and in a certain class of establishment - what, in those days, was seen as the supreme importance of the proprietor, or the maître d'hôtel. In essence, this was the cult of the 'front man'. He was the prime attraction, as opposed to 'the chef', for he was a back-room worker. Thus, at high class establishments across Europe, the businesses were very dependent on the personality of the front man. That rule of personal identity has not changed over the years and he suggested: 'If he, the name behind the establishment is there, business is good but he has to be present to give it that individuality for which people will go there, and that individuality will be recognised because of him and him alone.

'It is no good giving a place a name of a famous celebrity (be it a famous chef or otherwise) and hoping that the magic of an absentee proprietor with a famous name will be enough, for in the long run that will not be the case.'

Robin Seymour has touched on a very big subject there. The passing years have seen the change in emphasis with the decline of the main focus of the restaurant actually being in the front for meeting and greeting, whereas the current fashion is for the name over the door being actually out of sight in the kitchen.

There is also a trend towards eatery chains (one hesitates to say 'franchising'), with the name selling the establishment - even if, as Robin implied, the name is never, or at least hardly ever, there. Indeed, the involvement of the famous name can sometimes be limited to advice on styling, a recipe book and offering a benediction from afar.

Tino Rossi has recently celebrated his 50 years as the highly visible proprietor and front man at his Halkett Place restaurant, La Capannina. His customers take his presence as essential as they also do the presence and influence of his wife Ida. That said, the most universal way of referring to the establishment is by his name as in: 'We're off to Tino's for dinner this evening.' The same was true with Victor at the Sea Crest, Mirto at the Moorings and Mauro, first at the Old Court House in Gorey, then at his restaurant in La Motte Street. These four Grand Old Men of Italian restaurateurs set the tone for the Island. They all welcomed their regular customers by name, and somehow implied that it would not have been worth opening if they had not arrived. They would made a fuss when taking the order and, then like true professionals, stood back and leave them to enjoy their evening out while basking in the warmth of a good welcome.

I myself experienced that powerful force in action when my father, who had moved back to London for a time, came over to Jersey on business and offered to take me out with the words: 'Let's go and see Mauro at the Old Court House.' Mauro had moved and my father's information was ten years out of date. Explaining the situation to Mauro, he managed to squeeze us in to his new, smaller, restaurant and, on arrival, nodded to me then turned to my Father with the words: 'Mr Crosby it has been a long time.'

My immediate reaction was to think: 'Mauro, what a performance, but you only knew that because I told you three days ago.' But that didn't matter for, on reflection, he had remembered the details behind that booking through three days of busy service and meeting his existing customers. Furthermore that little phrase put my father in an excellent mood because: 'Mauro remembered me after all these years!' It would not have mattered what had been served that evening, my father was pre-disposed to enjoy it, thanks to this example of true professionalism.

Mauro had set up his restaurant in La Motte Street as a double act with Irene, who sat at reception, prepared the bills and, of course, was the first face of the restaurant when a guest arrived. He had perfected his skills as a restaurant manager at the Old Court House in Gorey where he would have to balance the demands of the dining room against the demands of management. As he discovered, a good hotelier knew when to stand back and let his maître get on with the job.

Looking back, Mauro remembers the excellent relationship he built up with the late Don Hoare at the Old Court House. But there came the time when Don had to go to hospital leaving his wife Pam in charge and so his father came down to keep an eye on things. According to Mauro, Mr Hoare (senior) put his nose into every aspect of the hotel and was driving many of the staff mad, including his daughter-in-law Pam. As he remembers, she was in an embarrassing position as she couldn't order her father-in-law around and so she begged him to say something. 'Leave it to me,' he said.

The next day Mauro waited until they were both at breakfast then, after the polite good morning, took him to one side and said: 'You don't have to do a thing while your son is away. The chef knows his job, I know my job, Mrs Hoare is in charge of the office staff and she knows her job, so leave us alone. Stay here, talk to the customers, make them welcome and enjoy your food.

'He looked at me a moment then nodded and sat down without saying a word. During the rest of his stay we all got on with our work and Pamela Hoare was very grateful.'

But you can only do that from a position of strength gained through knowing you are doing a good job and furthermore, that you have no outstanding or unresolved matters with the owner.

Tino Rossi epitomises those times for, when he started, the important guy who waved the flag for an establishment, restaurant or smart hotel dining room was the maître d'hôtel. He made sure the customers were well treated and provided the theatrical backdrop to an evening out. 'Going out was more than food on a plate. But the chef is king now.'

Tino was schooled while travelling with the big brigades to many different hotels. He explained that the maître had to work closely with the chef so that the kitchen and the dining room could work together and that the service was planned and delivered. 'But I think that deep down, the chef was always second to the top maître and that's why, in the public's view, the maîtres were the really big names at the Savoy, the Dorchester, the Ritz and the other great establishments.'

However, the new generation of chef superstars didn't want maîtres anymore; they wanted to do it all themselves. As Tino said: 'They produce luxury trattoria food; everything on the plate. It looks good; it is presented beautifully and imaginatively. But has it got what I think a good meal should have - and that includes a proper welcome and service? I don't know.'

But what were the hotels whose service and style the Italians who came to Jersey brought with them? Before he arrived in Jersey to work at Hotel L'Horizon, the late Giuseppe Francescon spent seasons working in Switzerland as well as Venice.

He recalled his time in the Gstaad Palace which he remembers as one of the most beautiful hotels in the world. 'It was an attraction for all the famous people who would come and stay there,' he once said, saying that he had been flabbergasted when he first saw it, standing there like a Cinderella castle. 'I enjoyed that whole experience very much,' he was to say at a later date. 'Gstaad catered for the celebrities of the time and they all came to the Palace. Of course, there were other hotels but the Palace, which had been specially built as a sumptuous hotel was, and remains, definitely a special place; in fact I would say the special place of Gstaad and therefore of Switzerland.'

Gstaad is a village in the German-speaking section of the Canton of Bern in south-western Switzerland. It has long been known as a popular destination among high society and the international jet set as a major ski resort. The Gstaad Palace opened in 1913 as its first luxury hotel and the staff there catered for the whims of an astonishing array of celebrities of the time, as well as the stars who were brought there to entertain them. Gala dinners with international artistes were the highlights of the winter seasons during the 1960s. Marlene Dietrich performed at one such event and the list of celebrity guests and entertainment legends is long and diverse. It included names such as Louis Armstrong, Benny Goodman and Ella Fitzgerald, Maurice Chevalier, Gilbert Bécaud, Dionne Warwick and Petula Clark.

Giuseppe remembered some of them - people who - a young man like him - had only read about. He recalled seeing and serving Gunter Sachs and Brigitte Bardot, Richard Burton and Elizabeth Taylor, Maurice Chevalier and when he was there, Johnny Mathis was singing as was Mireille Mathieu. 'Princess Soraya, the wife of the Shah of Persia, was a guest there,' he remembered. 'In fact she was living permanently there at the time, as I suppose she was not getting on with her husband. Oh yes, and David Niven was there also - one of my favourites, a fantastic gentleman. Do you know, in real life he seemed exactly the same as he was in the movies.'

In such a location as the Palace one must wonder whether these ultra-famous people, so used to having every whim catered for and their surroundings planned accordingly, actually noticed the staff. Perhaps the waiters were just part of the hotel's fixtures and fittings; a type of human wallpaper.

Not really, according to Giuseppe; at least not as he remembered it. They hardly became best friends, but in a sense he looked back on the staff being quite involved, not just hovering around in the background. He spoke of the several restaurants in the hotel: 'I was working in the Grill. It was a small, highly select, à la carte restaurant with a small band playing discretely at the end of the room. There were only a dozen or so tables, so it was a very small place and, certainly when I was there, seems to have been one of the chosen meeting places for the rich and famous. Being small and intimate the patrons would recognise and talk to some of the staff. I was doing what I was trained for and I had a fantastic time. How could I not enjoy it?'

But there were other considerations apart from star-gazing such as the chance of travel, promotion and broad experience. These were all high on his agenda, as was the case for all those ambitious young men from Italy who travelled the world and came to Jersey. So, having enjoyed his experience of the celebrity culture in Switzerland, he returned to Jersey and the Hotel L'Horizon.

As Giuseppe recalled in an interview, 'yes I first came to Jersey in 1966 then I went to Gstaad in 1968 before coming back to Hotel L'Horizon. It was a little bit different to what it is now as it was, without doubt, the most prestigious hotel in Jersey. Every night there was a dinner dance I remember. The restaurant was always full - choc-a-bloc - yes it was a very nice place to be and a great place to work.'

A great place to work? Derek Maltwood, a former director of L'Horizon recalls the ethos of the hotel. 'The staff members were like a big family. I remember as a young lad going to the inter-hotel football matches. The non-playing staff and their families were all there to support the team and even the hotel band came along, adding to the noise on the touch-line. And don't forget the island-wide influence of the Maître Aldo Valli and Chef Piero Alzetta who acted, in effect, as an introduction (and a filter at the same time) for some of the best Italian talent into the Island. The hotel was a huge influence.'

Another Jersey Italian to experience the celebrity culture of Switzerland's famous hotels, albeit a decade before Giuseppe Francescon, was Tino Rossi. But as he stressed, you could not, as a young Italian, up sticks and go to Switzerland to look for work. In those days, the only way to do it was with a brigade.

Tino was one of the many generations of Italians who chose the catering trade as a way of travelling, improving their lives and earning money far in excess of what could have been achieved at home. The young boy, who had carried messages for the partisans, finished school at 15 as he wanted to leave and seek his fortune away from the village. As he viewed it then, it was stuck miles from anywhere, way up near the Yugoslavian border in north-eastern Italy. He knew he had to travel, as it was very difficult to find any work otherwise. Traditionally, there had been many people from his village who worked in hotels, so he used all those contacts to help him find the right opening: 'It took me a long time to find a good place but, from then on, that was it, my way forward was decided.'

He explained that it took a long time, because it was essential to try very hard to get into the best brigade that he could find. That meant applying to the best and most famous maître you could approach. 'And the better, the more elite brigade you could join meant that you had greater opportunities to advance and improve your prospects and therefore your career in general.'

He spent time moving around the big hotels in top resorts such as St Moritz or Montreux in the winter and Venice in the summer and, as was the case with Giuseppe, it was inevitable that he dealt with many famous people. That was the celebrity culture of the time and those were the places he was working in.

Reading back-copies of newspapers and high life magazines of the time, the celebrities were royals: kings, queens, duchesses and grand dukes of various countries. Switzerland seemed to be a permanent nesting place for many of these famous people. Tino remembers: 'Yes, especially in the winter time when you worked in St Moritz, the Palace for example. Apart from the Royals, you would also be serving the Agnellis and other famous families. Then there were the movie stars and playboys; the Shah of Persia was often there, the Aga Khan and all the big names, because in those days they didn't go away from Europe as much as they do now, not because they couldn't afford it, but because of the lack of facilities elsewhere - facilities that they deemed suitable and fashionable enough at least.'

But some of them were very demanding and were so removed from real life that they had no consideration for the people who served them. For example, King Farouk, if you were to believe what was reported, spent more time in the top hotels than he did in Egypt.

According to Tino he was quite a headache for the staff. He would arrive at the hotel and take the whole second floor, then seal it off with body guards and, as Tino put it, 'all sorts of strange characters'. It was not uncommon for one of his entourage to be sent to get some temporary girlfriend or whatever might be needed and then King Farouk would vanish into some form of separate universe emerging only to order a full dinner at six o'clock in the morning and breakfast at four o'clock in afternoon.

'We had to have kitchen and service on standby 24-hours-a-day,' said Tino. 'And King Farouk would decide what to eat at whatever time he felt like it and expect everything delivered immediately, or at least to be prepared immediately.' It was not, Tino remembers, a question of having to be dragged out of bed to satisfy some strange comestible whim, for the King's presence was merely another complicated rota for the maître to arrange on top of all his other duties: 'For us it was work when you had to, sleep when you could, and try to keep your balance the rest of the time.'

Keeping your balance indeed; one thing was certain; being in the front line for this sort of service was not a place for learners - young commis waiters. It was not a question of spilling sauce over a priceless fur or evening gown for, unless you were good at your job, the maître d'hôtel or his assistant running that station would not allow you anywhere near the guests.

'I once had a very embarrassing accident with a large serving tray of food,' Tino remembered. 'I tripped over a thick rug that someone had put in the middle of the room since I had last been there. So that was another useful lesson to add to my list. Try very hard not to fall over with a tray of food more than once in front of King Farouk,' he recalled with a smile.

The dining rooms in this class of hotel (be it in Gstaad, where Giuseppe Francescon worked, or in Montreux or in any of the great hotels of Europe) were highly structured with the maître d'hôtel ensuring that his assistant maîtres and everyone down to the commis de suite bringing the food to the gueridon were working with a high degree of synchronisation. At every good hotel, be it in Venice, Gstaad or in St Brelade's Bay, there was at that time an overriding objective, serve it hot. 'Quand vous servez la merde,' snarled one Swiss hotel manager to a junior Italian demi chef de rang, who had left the food he had just cooked unattended and cooling on the gueridon for a minute too long, 'servez la merde chaude!'

'Of course that was in the days the people liked their food hot, not tiede (lukewarm),' said Tino. 'Everything had to be very hot; you used to say you could tell a successful waiter by the calluses or burn marks on his fingers from permanently handling very hot dishes and plates.'

One would have thought that the comparison from smart fashionable upper class Europe grand hotels to Jersey would have been severe, but after that glimpse of the high life, how did Tino first react to Jersey when he first came over in the 1950s?

'I don't know the word, but it was more moderate compared to what we had seen in Switzerland, Venice and so on. But it was very nice and we could see that there would be more promising, more possibilities for us to express ourselves and be appreciated.'

After his spell in Switzerland, Giuseppe Francescon noticed the difference: 'In all honesty, after working in Switzerland where the standards were so high and in Germany which was up there as well, it was a bit of a shock to the system, as Jersey was in some respects a bit antiquated back then.' But, like anywhere else in a new job, Giuseppe just had to get used to the new place, get used to the way things were done and then make the best of it.

And make the best of it they did. It is a point that bears repeating, for those who succeeded made us in Jersey realise the essential difference between successful Italian businessmen on the one hand and on the other hand, successful businessmen who happened to be Italian. Victor Cornaglia agrees whole-heartedly with this sentiment: 'Yes, an important distinction and one that makes Jersey a nice place to live. We have all gone at things in different ways. Me, Tino, Mauro for example, the so-called three musketeers chose one direction. Giancarlo Mattioli, for example, although he arrived and worked in the catering business made a success out of property - and well done to him. The important point is that we had freedom to do that because we were accepted.'

He continued: 'I think one of the ways we appealed to people was the way we could compose a menu for special events. The praise was universal. And the letters I have received and the compliments about menus I had arranged; Tino and Mauro will tell you the same.'

'The other great thing about us three musketeers in particular (or to be fair, any Italians who ran a successful dining room), was that we were real professionals, for we knew when to stop. Be effusive with the welcome, make a fuss over the orders, and then stand back.'

One evening at some Italian event I overheard Victor talking to Tino and Mauro. They had an overlap of customers - especially the business customers, for those were the days of long expense accounts and even longer lunches. Victor said: 'I don't object, but have you noticed how so many of them have come to expect a drink on the house at the end of the meal or even a glass of champagne before. I have never been to any of their banks and been offered a five pound note as a gesture of appreciation. Have you?'

To be to be a professional who leads a dining room requires an extensive background in learning the skills, as we have discovered. Giancarlo Mattioli said that being a waiter in Italy is a profession in many ways. He said you had to know not only about serving food but also being able to prepare it and, in certain situations, cook it. Also, you had to master arcane skills, such as being able to peel a grape with a fork and a knife - and we have already heard from Maurizio Marzana about peeling and presenting an orange. 'These things are not easy, believe you me,' said Giancarlo, 'but it can be done and we did it because that is what we were trained to do in hotels in Italy and I worked in several big hotels in the season.'

The success of the Italian influx into the Jersey catering industry saw the new generation of diners struggling to come to grips with the new style of continental cooking and food presentation. Everyone can remember, sometimes with deep embarrassment, the first time they were exposed to a new food especially one which required some new, and as it seemed, sophisticated, method of eating it properly. It was a quiet revolution in many ways, for this whole period provided, across the hotels and restaurants, a culinary education for English diners of new tastes, new recipes and new ways of serving food.

If this is really the case, it gets to reinforce the feeling expressed by many of my older friends, who said that not only the leading professionals of the time, but also all the Italians who were fronting up the many cafés and restaurants that sprung up in Jersey, taught the Island how to eat. If that's an exaggeration, it is an understandable one. In my case, it would contain a strong element of fact.

But perhaps it was not only the Jersey diners who benefited from that knowledge brought in by those who had worked up through the brigade system. One can summarise the views of Giancarlo - which coincide with those of Paulo Crolla, who came to Jersey about 18 years later. They would admit that their elder and more experienced colleagues taught them and their own particular age groups the necessary skills to advance in their chosen careers.

Giancarlo recalled: ‘This is especially true in methods of lamp work, flambé, which became ever more popular during that time. At the end of the meal, people just had to have a *crêpe suzette* or a *banane flambé* and a young man like me would watch them being prepared. We would not be let loose on a customer’s food when we were young and inexperienced, but gradually these older men passed on their skills and so they gave us the chance to prove ourselves and we learnt - we had to learn, very quickly.’

It was a sense of theatre and it added to the experience of dining out. But, of course, with the development of cuisine and the change in style and emphasis, people these days would not expect that sort of service. As a result, some might argue, the professionalism and range of responsibilities for waiting staff have, in a sense, been reduced.

It is an unfortunate fact Giancarlo argued that, like all trades, catering - away from the top restaurants - is being simplified. ‘You add to that the obvious truth (to me at any rate), that people are always in a hurry, meals are being cut short and the endless rise of simple fish and chip type bars and take-away restaurants, not only in Jersey but internationally, concerns me. People might be regressing in their food appreciation.’

His advice would be: ‘Be more concerned with the quality of food, its preparation and service and waste a little more time eating at a table. But the restaurants that continue to give good food still show Italian dishes and specialities that are not only typically Italian but also, now, typically British, because not all Italian restaurants have focussed exclusively on their own culinary heritage.’

Victor Cornaglia happy in retirement

Chapter 7

PROGRESS

THE Italians who chose to come to Jersey and make their career in the Island originally came for a variety of reasons. Of these, the most compelling was the desire to find better paid work than was available back in Italy, combined with the desire to travel and gain language skills.

Also, the long established tradition of travelling to find work in catering was still very much alive and there was a wide selection of hotel schools and/or catering colleges in Italy that could impart not only the basic skills, but also install the belief that the career path they were choosing was both professional and respected.

That, combined with the influence of the brigades in hotel dining, assured that travel was relatively simple if you worked your contacts. Furthermore, getting attached to a good maître d'hôtel ensured that the process of learning continued as the pursuit of excellence was presumed. The onus placed on the young waiters to be proficient in the language of their host country gave confidence to the young men, on what little time off they could muster, to socialise outside their immediate circle, as they were able to communicate with the local population. Indeed, many 'Jersey Italians' met and married girls who were not Italian; they could have been Jersey or, in many cases, from the United Kingdom.

Settling down in their adopted country with a British wife gave them a wider, more panoramic, vision beyond the attainment of what would have been their original aim: to do well in the brigade and perhaps rise to the dizzy heights of maître. Other considerations now applied when they realised that there was life beyond the brigade or even the dining room, and there were other paths to doing well.

Of overriding importance now they were married, was the realisation they could, with hard work, give their children a better start in adulthood, with more choices than they themselves had been given back in Italy. The big break was there - and it could come from having one's own business. There was often a growing desire to be one's own boss and the final push to leave the protection of paid employment, albeit at a high level, and strike out on one's own. This could come from a variety of sources, none more individual than the origin of the encouragement given to the late Giuseppe Francescon.

Giuseppe rose to the top of his profession, being maître d'hôtel at Hotel L'Horizon, then one of Jersey's premier hotels, and winning the trophy for the 1989 Head Waiter of the Year across the whole of the United Kingdom: 'That was something I am very proud of. There were entrants from Ireland, Scotland and Wales as well as England and I came out top.' And he had every justification for being proud, for there also was in Gio's, his Halkett Place restaurant, a picture of him, impeccably turned out, being presented to the Queen.

He once told me that the picture dated from 1989, which he described as 'the year that everything happened' to him. That was the year of a Royal Visit of Her Majesty to Jersey, during which he was presented to her, not only as the man who had supervised the service at a large formal lunch organised by the Bailiff and the States, but also as the recipient of the accolade 'Head Waiter of the Year' in the United Kingdom. During the presentation they had a short conversation. The story is best told in Giuseppe's own words.

'That was, as I said, in 1989, but I also looked after Her Majesty in the late 1970s when she came to Jersey. After the meal I was in the line up to be presented to her and we had a little chat. She asked if I had been drafted in for a special occasion or was I still working at the hotel full-time. How she knew all about me I don't know, but obviously she had been well briefed and well prepared.

'Yes, Your Majesty,' I replied, 'I am still here.'

'But you should be working for yourself,' she said.

'Thank you very much Your Majesty I am actually very happy where I am.'

'No, no,' she said, 'you should be working for yourself, you would be very successful.'

'Thank you very much for your advice Your Majesty. I will go home and speak to my wife about it.'

'So, within two months I had this restaurant. Obviously, once it had opened, I had to send her a little note saying, in effect, thank you very much for your advice which I took, and now I have my own restaurant. I got a little reply saying my communication had been noted and made available to Her Majesty.'

He did not have the same exalted inspiration as Giuseppe but, in a sense, Maurizio Marzana's career followed a similar path in that it mirrored the changes of Jersey tourism and indeed mirrored, therefore, the dining habits of the world at large. He had started by working across Europe for smart and fashionable hotels with large multi-station dining rooms and even larger function rooms, and his aim was to get to the top of that profession and see the world. But just when he made it to the top he stepped sideways and for nearly 30 years, like so many of his colleagues, was running his own business, being a joint owner of a small hotel/guest house, which was also a very busy informal restaurant, in St Aubin; the Bon Viveur. For nearly ten years he worked there in partnership with Angelo Mariani and then with Enzo Savarese.

Maurizio's success, in conjunction with his business partners at the Bon Viveur, reflects the way tourism in Jersey itself has changed from a time when the regulations insisted that there should be as many seats in the dining room as there were beds in the hotel as most meals were eaten in house. The fashion changed to more informal arrangements as many tourists would choose to vary where they ate and often only reserved their stay with a bed and breakfast booking.

Accepting that there was a parallel between his career and the changing nature of Jersey Tourism, Maurizio said that, at some time in life, everyone has to sit down and work out, or perhaps re-assess, what their aims were: 'You start in catering school and you leave as a commis waiter with some basic skills. You then want to become a chef de rang, then an assistant head waiter, then restaurant manager but once you reach the top of that particular ladder you have to work out if there is a next step somewhere and, if so, is it one you can take.'

'I became the restaurant manager and in charge of dining at functions at the Grand Hotel; it would have been difficult to go much higher but I couldn't just call a halt to my career development at that stage. If I were to take that path I would have to spend too many years ahead of me just going through the motions, efficiently, but without drive or passion.'

As Maurizio saw it, the only other option, if you want to use your skills and not change direction completely is to reach out in a different way with your own business and you can match it to your own ideas and own personality. 'I left the Grand in 1982 and I have been working for myself since then. There are many other pressures and responsibilities but there is no general manager or owner imposing his view on how things should be done. I can do what I feel is best for the customer and the business and keep up-to-date with the trends I want to follow in what is now a very fractured market.'

And, of course, with that move to more informal dining came the lessening of importance of the traditional maître d'hôtel. There was a time when the famous maîtres of old at the Dorchester, the Savoy or other grand hotels were the ultimate arbiters of taste. Just a suspicion of a raised eyebrow was enough to make the most self-centred guest quail. And on that subject, I was present one evening when Tino Rossi threw out, or perhaps refused entry would be more exact, a one-time very famous television cook; Fanny Craddock. This was not because she criticised his food in a review, that was her prerogative, but because she was also rude about his staff and Italians in general. And I thought at the time when I witnessed the exchange: 'Well done, that's a man who stands up for his own.'

Tino remembered the occasion well. 'Yes that was true, we had some strong and also inappropriate criticism from this lady and then one day, not long afterwards, she arrived out of the blue demanding a table. "Don't you know who I am?" Well if I had a pound for every time I have heard have that phrase I would have retired long ago. I wasn't impressed so I said to the boys make her wait. Anyway, I eventually went up to her and said there was no table for her in this restaurant saying; "you can criticise the cooking in this restaurant but you were unnecessarily insulting to me and the staff; that is unacceptable". "The man's impertinent," she exclaimed and stormed out. It had all been very public, so I was slightly worried, but after she left, I got a big round of applause from all the diners, so I am glad I decided to stand up to her ego.'

But Victor Cornaglia was well on his way to becoming a grand old maître of the London dining scene, having been employed as a head waiter in the Savoy Hotel River Room. So, to an outsider, it might seem strange to give up that privileged position to return to Jersey.

When Victor was in Jersey running the dining room at the Water Edge, he got to know the late Frank Thomasson as a regular customer. Frank also used to come to the Savoy in London so he maintained the connection. The Lobster Pot Restaurant at L'Etacq was for sale and Frank wanted to buy it but only if he could persuade Victor and his wife Ida to come and run it. As Victor explained, 'through mutual friends Frank got hold of me one evening late at night when we were at a birthday party.

It was 11.30, very late, when a call came through and I thought it was somebody winding me up. It was all very noisy and confused and I was repeating the essence of the conversation over my shoulder to Ida and she told me to say 'Yes' and hang up. We both thought it was a drunken joke.'

Three days later Victor was called to the staff manager's office at the Savoy who had been told he was going to Jersey: 'What for?' Victor asked.

'To manage the Lobster Pot,' was the reply.

'Oh my God it wasn't a joke,' he said.

It turned out that a lawyer from Jersey had been to the Hotel to get a reference so that the license application for the Lobster Pot could go through with Victor's name as the manager. That was Advocate Dick Cristin. Victor wasn't sure about any move as he was happy at the Savoy and Ida was happy working in reception at Quaglino's. 'I went to phone her and by the time I got back to the office, still undecided, Sir Hugh Wontner's secretary rang me up and told me to come up and see her.'

Sir Hugh was managing director of the Savoy hotel group from 1941 to 1979 and its chairman from 1948 to 1984, continuing as president until his death. He restored the Savoy Group to its pre-eminence after the war and successfully preserved its independence against take-over bids throughout his career.

'The secretary told me she had heard all the conversation and had cleared an offer for me: they would release me and I would go to Jersey for two years. By then the new Berkeley would be built at Knightsbridge and I would come back as the new restaurant manager.' Victor was told that such a move would give him the necessary good management experience needed for his proposed promotion to the Berkeley.

By the late 60s and into the 70s the Italian transformation of the catering industry was deeply entrenched but, even then, the ability to be surprised with something new served up by an enterprising Italian was always there. And, as Eric Ruaro remembers, there were always plenty of places who would serve no matter what was required, even if, in his words, 'all you wanted was overdone steak and sloppy pasta.'

'Saturday remained, in many restaurants, the night out for the well done steak and chip brigade. I remember in 1975 in the Ancient Harbour at

St Aubin, I featured tortellini and no one knew what it was. I also used to make a lasagne as it is done in Italy. It is cooked in a large dish from which came nice square portions that held their own shape when sitting on the plate. Some diners would look at it in surprise and complain that it was not lasagne. The lasagne they were used to, and so what they were expecting and wanted, would be sloppy and almost a soup. No that's being rude about soup; something like thick wallpaper paste was what they were looking for.'

Indeed, I was living in St Aubin then and remember being in that restaurant as a customer at the time that the chef (Eric) came out of the kitchen bearing a large knife and looking very fierce while demanding: 'Who is complaining about MY lasagne?' It was the first time I met him.

When Tino Rossi heard that story his reaction was that there was nothing unusual about it: 'Some chefs, in those days, would come in to the restaurant if called for, with a knife, pretending they had been disturbed while busy chopping herbs and had brought it with them by mistake. I didn't mind, it was a good warning to customers about pushing their luck.'

Right from the early days of La Capannina, Tino had no choice other than to source some of his ingredients from off the Island in order to meet his claim to be an Italian restaurant. As and when more products became available, the menu adapted and changed. However, it always avoided being a pizza and pasta house; he had a much broader vision.

Part of the reason for that stance was his background. He said he had always worked in high quality restaurants and hotels and, in those rarefied environments, pizza was never considered as a restaurant food. Tino maintained that the pizza explosion came later when it was re-invented by the Americans and sent back to Europe. It was also a journey similar to that taken by cheesecake - but that's another story. 'Let's be honest,' he said, 'a pizzaiolo (a person who makes pizzas in a pizzeria) was never considered to be a chef. Nobody in those days could have approached a kitchen brigade and sought work as a pizzaiolo; they would have been shown the door. Now, of course, they are in great demand.'

But when Tino was building up his business into one of the premier eating spots in the Channel Islands, the emphasis was firmly on the front of house, on the welcome and so, for the customers arriving for an evening out, the emphasis was on a bit of theatre as well as going out for food. The flambés, the steak tartare being mixed at the table, the creation of a zabaglione, were all examples of that sense of a special and very visual treat.

'Flambés were always popular,' he said. '*Steak Diane* and *steak au poivre* were always available and part of the show. Theatre was required and we provided that. Sometimes, and I have managed to do it in recent years when we have our Italian week and I have a visiting chef from Italy, I would invite him out to do, or at least to finish, certain dishes in front of the table. The chef with his hat finishing the risotto at the table is part of the experience and, I must say, it was always well received.'

Tino remembers one chef, who spoke very good English. He also managed also to be an exceptional front man and he reminded those there during that week of what a sense of theatre was and how it added value to an evening out. 'It doesn't happen much now, but the younger generation, who perhaps have never seen a skilled maître d'hôtel at work, are genuinely surprised and delighted by what they see. Cooking in front of the people, or carving in front of the people; they are both something to watch, comment on and you look forward to the result. They get very excited and enthusiastic and then, obviously, are predisposed to enjoy the meal more.'

The carving trolley with the big joint of the day, saddle of lamb, suckling pig in season or even a selection of game at the appropriate time of the year, remains part of the reason for coming to the restaurant. Saddle of veal used to be a feature but, according to Tino, price now rules that out. Such was the popularity of the roast of the day as well as certain dishes that had to be prepared in front of the diners that no restaurateur could have survived by himself doing all the front of house work. For many years Tino was ably assisted by Carlo Ragazzi - another importation from Lake Maggiore - whose skill with a carving knife in particular was a joy to behold. Carlo eventually bought out Renato Volpe's share in the Restaurant de la Poste and joined Franco Gatti in a long running and successful business partnership.

It was earlier that Mauro had become one of the household names along with Tino and Victor and also Mirto. He had been the restaurant manager at the Old Court House in Gorey but when he opened his own restaurant, Mauro's, in 1972, his position at the top of the tree was assured as he eventually took his place in the line-up of the so-called three musketeers.

Mauro spent some time transforming what was once a simple café restaurant in La Motte Street and turning it into what he wanted it to be. During that period he used to meet Irene every Monday for lunch at La Capannina. 'One day I told Tino that as from the following week he would not be seeing me anymore. 'Yes,' he said, 'I had heard a rumour.' I told him: 'You are always complaining that you have to send customers away when you are full, so I will leave you the address and you will know where to send them. And we have been firm friends ever since.'

There was an occasion when going to see Mauro on a business matter back in the mid 1970s, I was reminded that restaurateurs have much in common with farmers inasmuch as they are never happy - always complaining about something. He was moaning that things were not so good as compared to the year before. I grabbed the big diary with all his bookings, flicked through a few days and said, 'you old misery, you are overbooked already for the next week. Look at the numbers; you even have a long waiting list.'

'Ah Hamish,' he replied. 'You don't understand. Last year I turned away many more people. Things are getting worse the whole time.'

The bane of the restaurateur's life in those times, in terms of ensuring a smooth flow of food out of the kitchen, was the drinking culture in the bar before a meal. Mauro recalls people wanting at least two drinks before they came through to dinner. 'You would announce a table was ready and then someone would say they would come in a couple of minutes, after another round. It was really annoying when the chef was trying to get the food coming out of the kitchen in a planned way, but you just had to smile and say whenever you are ready.'

The other feature was the extent of the range of drinks that had to be available, such as all the different aperitifs and spirit mixers; the idea of a glass of wine as an aperitif was unheard of in those days. And, after the meal, it was the same as a huge range of different liqueurs and spirits was expected. It was profitable albeit tricky to fit in with the running of a restaurant. A barman was kept very busy.

All this was possible, even in a far away restaurant such as the Lobster Pot, as there were no drink driving laws in Jersey during the 1960s and 1970s, or to put it another way, the police could not go out randomly breath-testing motorists. There had to be a reason to be tested and that normally meant after an accident.

At the time, every restaurant, good, bad or indifferent, had to prove its worth by offering what seemed to be an impossibly large menu and do the occasional flambé if asked. I remember a small hotel with a little restaurant that had spent some money meeting the new regulatory requirements, which published a double advertisement announcing its re-opening that read 'Flambés our speciality' and underneath a further push for the hotel restaurant that proclaimed: 'Fire precautions now complete.'

Eric Ruaro arrived at the end of the 1960s, towards the end, as some see it, of the great Italian invasion. Whether they were owners or managers, he says, the Italian influence was very important. He still believes that, overall, seen in terms of food and also of service, there was overall a better product on offer than now.

It was all very strictly run, largely by Italians, Eric remembers, and based on the old values as epitomised by the brigade. He doesn't forget the others who were there and their presence was very important, but the Italian influence prevailed in the dining room and in the kitchen. 'The food was correct and it had flair. Now, well perhaps I am being a bit of a grumpy old man, but I have been to some so-called good restaurants and the food is either tasteless or the good flavours are hidden by over-reliance on chilli so there is effectively no need for the chef to get the basics right.'

The good restaurants always maintained the ability to surprise with something new; it was a process of gradual change and not losing your market by dropping what was popular. I remember first seeing carpaccio in La Capannina and was amazed: 'Raw beef - really? What is going on here?' According to Tino: 'We all had to be a bit careful but the rise in foreign travel by the British helped them realise that, for example, carpaccio was a very good starter and it remains as popular as ever and even more popular in November when we get the white truffles.'

It was part of the permanent process of gradual change, and over the years Tino's annual celebration of Italian cuisine, involving bringing over a chef from Italy to prepare in a different way, regional specialities, has allowed him to introduce dishes that would be seen as normal now. Many local residents would recognise La Capannina as the place where they were first served carpaccio and shavings of white Alba truffle, black pasta, wild boar ham, not to mention old favourites such as vitello tonnato and zabaglione.

Although, of course, the young men from Italy arrived with experience and, in many cases, proper training, many still arrived in Jersey as young and relatively untried members of their profession. There remained skills to be learnt and knowledge to be imbued. According to Paulo Crolla, it wasn't a question of learning from a book or in a weekly class, it was a daily occurrence, a sort of culinary osmosis. Knowledge was absorbed despite the traditional rivalry between the dining room and kitchen staff.

He said he and his compatriots had a pride and passion concerning their jobs. He thought that, as a by-product of those qualities, he made many friends with his immediate colleagues, but it was never easy to make friends with those who worked in the kitchens. 'There was always friction between the two sides of the dining room service; in a way you could say that friendship stopped at the pass.'

He puts it down to pride as the chef would always want his food to be presented in the best possible way and, convinced that he was the best judge, would always blame the waiters if there were any problems or complaints. 'But for us in the dining room it was a good time,' he remembers. 'After the service we would go out together, clubs, discos, coffee bars as we were all close and liked each other's company. There we would exchange ideas and, if sometimes a little homesick, memories of Italy and home.'

The Italian community revolved around work and working practices; that was the cement that held it together rather than creating exiles' clubs. Those who were settling in and progressing in their careers had other things to do and think about; they were looking forward, making a new life, not hankering after a past that was becoming increasingly distant.

It is worth noting that Paulo said they used to meet up in clubs, discos, coffee bars, in other words they moved in the bigger world of local society rather than in a small cadre. And we can recall that Angelo Saccone married Rosemary, originally from Somerset, but was in Jersey working as a window dresser and they met at Lord's discotheque. Paulo himself married Allison who worked as a travel agency courier from Cardiff attached to Preston Travel locally. Paulo took over the Mary Rose Restaurant in Bath Street later in his career and it was Allison's Welsh background that gave it its very special twist, particularly on 1 March - St David's Day - an Italian serving a sauce made from Welsh laver bread makes the point.

Nevertheless, the Italians preserved an identity as a community of hard-working professionals. 'As I said, we were very close,' Paulo recalls. 'Even after work we would talk about how things were done and how much better we would do it if only someone gave us the chance. Our job and our responsibilities were both always there somehow and I don't think that is the same attitude today. Work does not spill over into your own time.' He gave, as an example, the fact that a watch was never needed at work as that started at the same time every day and continued until the service was finished, whenever that happened to be. 'That is how things have changed over the years. For us there had to be passion for the job, otherwise you would never have done it.'

But not all progress was in the same direction and the desire to set out on your own was always a powerful attraction. After eight years of residence, Giancarlo Mattioli was, in his words: 'free of permit'. This meant he could have a property and be free of control, other than those that applied to anyone in Jersey. The time had come to strike out, so he took a gamble and acquired the lease of the Café des Fleurs in New Street which became the Presto in 1967.

'I was, as we used to say "free of permit". I could rent or buy like a Jersey person or, and this was the path I took, starting my own business and at 28 with my own business, now it was time to work and work hard - but for myself and my family.'

The Café des Fleurs had been a tea room and Giancarlo set out to create something fast and simple that would appeal to as many people as possible. He decided that a straightforward three course meal for the working man would be the best plan. 'The word quickly got out and in a tiny kitchen we churned out hundreds of meals a day at 2/6d. There was soup or a juice, perhaps even a small salad and then roast beef, roast pork, lamb chop or an omelette. It was purposefully a very simple formula and that was a reflection on the kitchen, which was tiny, with very limited facilities. It was 6 by 6 with a sink, a cooker and a small fridge and that was it. It is just as well my wife is such a small girl.'

Apart from the menu of the day there were the usual standards that his customers would expect. Giancarlo recalls one Sunday, with only 24 covers and in a five-hour period he served 252 meals, be they a simple spaghetti Bolognese or even a mixed grill. They ran out of the three course meal options as there was not enough food in stock to deal with the demand. 'And can I tell you my wife was making the most perfect roast potatoes in Jersey at the time. They were a huge draw, people came especially for them, par boiled and then roasted; perfectly done.'

But traditions are hard to change, he remembers the most popular dish there over the week was sausage, egg, chips and beans; hardly - as he admitted - an Italian speciality. 'But that is what they wanted and I responded to my customers. I wasn't on a conversion trip; I had to cover my rent.'

It will never get into any culinary history book, but there was one dish that proved to be very popular and which combined English and Italian traditions in bizarre way. It came about three years later when the lease was renewed and the premises enlarged from 24 covers to 70. 'We named it after our home town and it was a strange Anglo-Italian combination: we named eggs Ferrarese. It was two eggs on two slices of toast covered in Antonietta's Bolognese sauce that she did so well. Nobody wanted sausage, egg, chips and beans from then on; they wanted the egg Bolognese as it became known!'

There was no accepted path for the Italians to pursue as they settled in their new home. Catering may have been the chosen path for many but that covered a multitude of possibilities ranging from the Savoy Hotel to a café in New Street; catering is a blanket term for a variety of activities. As Robin Seymour said earlier; 'the tourism industry in Jersey covered every type of activity. It was, in effect, a multi-layered beast. All visitors to Jersey had to be served no matter what their aspirations happened to be. We needed the stars, the celebrities, but in a hotel group like ours we needed the highly competent. We wanted knowledge, we wanted skill but, above all, we wanted them to run and work as a team in our dining rooms; competence, skill and the willingness to put the hotel first.'

Chapter 8

FURTHER PROGRESS

LOOKING at the Italians in Jersey as their careers progressed, it is important to remember where they came from and how they arrived, for that provides a clue as to where they finished. That is not, of course, taking into account the changes to their path through life brought about by embracing the possibilities offered by a society different from that in which they grew up.

As we have discovered, it was largely word of mouth that encouraged so many to come to Jersey. Someone knew someone else who had a friend who knew that so and so was looking to complete his brigade, and so the chain gradually extended and linked up. This certainly seems to have been the way for seasonal hotels, where the owner could say: 'I don't have to worry about the dining room as there is a head waiter there who knows what he is doing and will sort it out for me.' The head waiter would then rely on his own contacts, and then contacts of contacts, to fill the gaps.

It is a view of the times that Robin Seymour understands and with which he agrees, but only up to a point. He believed there was an aspect of cohesion to that approach that proved very valuable in terms of the brigade system and the advantages it delivered. 'You had trained staff, as you say, who could work together and wouldn't let someone who couldn't speak English near the guests. It would be a good idea to try it now in some places I think. The trouble was the better guys would often set off to open their own restaurants.'

It was for that reason he felt that the really top performers who became local celebrities were not the ones he wanted in his dining rooms. 'We wanted knowledge, we wanted skill, but we wanted them to work in and, of course run, a team with competence and willingness to put the hotel first.'

And in two of his hotels his wishes were certainly granted for the Pomme d'Or dining room was ruled over by Italo Miorin with the able assistance of Piero Alonghi and in the Seymour's newest hotel at the time, the Hotel de la Plage at Havre des Pas, they had the perfect man in Giacomo Riva. 'Unobtrusively good, he helped to bring out the best in the staff and was quietly and highly competent. He was an ideal front man in a place like La Plage, and with his excellent English he got on very well with the guests.'

The point about speaking English is echoed by many of the Italians for whom learning the language was one of the reasons they came to Jersey in the first place. The decline in this part of the service on offer is perhaps more apparent to them, as they remember the struggles of their early days, than it is to those for whom English is their first language. Eric Ruaro is one who gets frustrated by the apparent lack of ability, which he once described as lack of willingness, to communicate effectively.

He reminds us that when he arrived you were not allowed near a customer by the chef de rang unless you could speak enough English. As he said: 'You would get promoted if and when your English was good enough to have a sensible conversation with the customer and in my view that was absolutely correct.' He gives, as an example, what he says is the not-unusual experience of his wife Pat, who finds lack of English by the waiters a bit embarrassing when she goes out with her friends. 'They ask a simple question about a dish or enquire about something extra and the waiter does not understand what is being said. It doesn't help the enjoyment of going out to have a good time.'

He said that he found the catering trade very diverse now, which might or might not be a good thing. However, he recalled a time when he was asked to talk on a basic introduction course for hotel staff being run by Jersey Tourism. The implicit theme of the course was 'interacting with the customer' and so presenting Jersey in a good light. There were, as he remembered, quite a few different nationalities taking part.

'On the Monday I met the first group of 20 students who were all employed and working in the tourism industry in positions that included dealing directly with their customers. Out of that group nearly half could speak hardly a word of English and I was amazed. How could they give good service to a customer when they don't understand what the customer wants or is trying to say to you? Those sorts of standards would simply not have been acceptable in Jersey at the time when I came over.'

The problem that was always there in terms of staffing was the Tourism Law in Jersey, which stipulated that a hotel had, by law, to offer full board and have as many seats in the main dining room as was necessary to allow everyone staying at the hotel to sit and eat at the same time. That requirement, by definition, put a strain on any staffing arrangements, in particular, of course, the rota.

It wasn't just the dining room; each bath had to be at least a minimum length, each wardrobe so high and so wide - on it went. Robin Seymour felt that people might wonder, when viewed from today, at such attention to detail by the authorities, but the tourism sector had grown so large so quickly that some form of control was absolutely essential.

'You didn't have to market the Island; the visitors came pouring in and unless the Tourism Committee stood their ground on basic standards and instituted some system of control, it could have gone out of control. This could only be achieved through the grading system; it was a pity in a way. The big trouble was,' he continued, 'that a whole department grew up based on control, definition and enforcement and they did not know, when it became necessary to switch from control to promotion, how to change emphasis and they left it a little late. By the 1980s that was the big problem with Jersey Tourism which, for two to three years (some might say longer), hung on to their controls, which took their attention away from the changing world.'

During the late 1970s and beyond, the Italian community shrunk as many moved on or returned home to a new, economically successful Italy. They were replaced by other nationalities coming to fill the replacements needed to staff Jersey's tourism boom. Those Italians who stayed were highly visible as they tended to be the owner proprietors or the senior maîtres who Islanders, as a whole, soon came to recognise and, such is the way of these things, were pleased to be recognised in return.

My first sight of Mirto was at the Moorings. Going there to meet him, I was told he was at the back of the dining room dealing with the lobster tank, a fitting almost a *sine qua non* for a certain type of restaurant. I discovered that 'looking after the lobster tank' was a polite way of saying he was in bare feet and shorts inside the tank giving it a clean. Being set into a wall at the end of the room, the only way to do this was to go through a side door and then climb in from above. My first sight of Mirto at the Moorings, therefore, was a pair of legs, cut off above the knee and illuminated by the dim light of the dining room.

When Mirto was running the Moorings, it was one of the most popular establishments to eat in Jersey. For a short time there were four places at the top of the where-to-eat list: Tino at La Capannina; Victor, who made his name at the Lobster Pot and then created the Sea Crest; Mauro, who eventually had his own restaurant in La Motte Street after making a huge success at the Old Court House in Gorey, and Mirto at the Moorings.

It was an example of the way the person at the front made such a difference in those days for that is who you went to see; the man, not the place. It was also an illustration of the importance of the Italians in the restaurant scene.

Not that they had it all their own way; there were other local restaurateurs, the Sharps at the Old Court House in St Aubin as well as George Skelley at the Bistro Borsalino in St Helier. It was not long before the success of the Borsalino in Cattle Street encouraged George to create a family and the Bistro Frere opened in St Martin and that was followed by the Bistro Soleil (a pun on 'son of Bistro') at Beaumont as well as a bistro overseas in Guernsey's St Peter Port. Finally, the last to open and the last to close, many years later and run by George's widow, Rosie, was the Borsalino Rocque at Grouville.

Nevertheless, the Italians had a visibility and a success above their numbers for, as a community, they punched well above their weight. Other Italians who owned and/or ran restaurants could be found at the Belmonte, Gio's, the Steak House, La Poste, Mino's, the Mont Orgueil as well as the Bon Viveur, Mary Rose, Mona Lisa, La Barca, La Buca, Luigi's, Isola Bella and most recently the Vecchia Milano and La Cantina, to name but a few. As a sign of the times the decision, in the early 1980s, by Bruno Zunino and his business partner Bruno Pesco to upgrade the Cup and Saucer café at Charing Cross and turn it into a quality restaurant, La Taverne, illustrates the way Jersey changed. Opening the new restaurant, Bruno Pesco said to me that they hoped for a good summer trade with the tourists to see them through a quiet winter. Now that is no longer the case for La Taverne relies heavily on the local market.

One quality that these restaurants had in common, apart from the Italian ownership and/or management, was that none of them in those days was a pizza-pasta house. They were all Italian and French in influence - European restaurants, in effect. The first modern pizzeria was the Pizza Express in Halkett Place, which opened in the early 1970s and was part of a national franchise.

Of course, there were also the Grill Rooms at the Grand Hotel with Augusto in charge, and The Star Grill at L'Horizon with Sandro Tiboni, which stood out, as did Lino di Meo at the Atlantic and Leo di Biasi at the St Brelade's Bay. Then there was the whole group of successful hoteliers who made their names as managers, and the contribution made by this group - that included Mario Dugini and Sylvano Cavicchia at the Atlantic and Woodville hotels, respectively - should never be forgotten in any review of the Italian contribution to tourism.

But no list would be complete without mention of the most un-Italian sounding restaurant; that was the Apple Cottage in Rozel. This was the domain of Settimo (Setti) Pozzi whom we first met when he came over to Jersey, with Renzo Martin, at the urging of Mirto Sappé. He started at the Hotel Corona but left to progress his career elsewhere. Working the season in Jersey and the winter months in the UK for a few years he met and later married his wife to be, Patricia, when working in Leeds. She followed him back to Jersey where they married and made the Island their home.

He became head chef at the Savoy Hotel and, with Patricia, taking it over and managing the business in 1971 when John Gay retired. In 1981 they took the risk of buying the Apple Cottage tea rooms at Rozel and turning it into a restaurant. This soon became a popular destination in the bay for visitors as well as locals and his customers included a string of local and visiting celebrities. He was one of the Grand Old Men of the Italian community and was never too proud to learn more about his craft. Having sold the Apple Cottage, he used to help out Tony Dorris the executive chef at the Jersey Pottery kitchens as he wanted to learn more about the modern trends of cooking and presentation. However, ill health caught up with him before he could put that into practice for himself, and he died in 2009. Another link to the past was broken.

These restaurants flourished in the era when directors had better things to do in the afternoon than sit in an office; that was why the staff were employed. The local good restaurant was where many a deal was struck. Anyone with business antennae in working order needed only to look at the tables at Mauro's ('Coopers and Lybrand's canteen' as it was known) or La Capannina at lunchtime in St Helier; in that way they could find out which companies had cause to celebrate a success, or who was planning some major expansion or joint action.

The best of the bunch were recognised meeting venues and long-lunch discussion places; the head of the Transport Union, René Liron, and the head of the major local supermarket group, Dick Riches, or the managing director of the brewery, Ian Steven, used them to hammer out wage settlements for the next year. Each side knew each other well, and also liked and respected each other, but they were on opposite sides and no holds were barred in the annual tussle. But at least it took place in civilised surroundings.

However, the days of the Bailiff's permit were over and there was no law which said that Italians had no choice other than to work in catering. So it was that those who saw a chance of change took it. As we have seen, Angelo Saccone, wanting to see more of his new wife and family, opted for a more nine-to-five existence by going in to retail. Others opened their own businesses or worked with wholesalers or moved across into finance, which had overtaken agriculture in size as a contributor to the Jersey's Gross National Product and was rapidly catching up with tourism.

Giancarlo Mattioli's major interest changed from working in, to owning the building itself: The Casablanca, for example, and nowadays the Marina at Havre des Pas, rather than the daily grind of catering. However, he did not disown his background; for example he remains a member of AMIRA (see chapter 10). Mirto was soon to leave the Moorings just before the change in ownership; he became a director of Bass Charrington and took on the food franchise at their busiest outlet, the Harvest Barn. He also took time to develop his own wine company, Gorey Wine Company, and after a great success at the Harvest Barn, took over the catering franchise at the Jersey Museum.

Eric Ruaro moved into wine wholesaling after the Ancient Harbour and a spell being a partner at an Italian tailor, while others bought guest houses, thus providing themselves with alternative work or, in many cases, a good income from the rental. However, their success in becoming the visible face of the catering industry in Jersey had fixed the public perception as to what they, as a nation, could do best.

But it wasn't just the well-known restaurants that provided a good living for those who owned or ran them. The smaller cafés, such as the Coffee Cup and La Toscana, did well as did others such as the Café Presto. But for a long time, there was also one place that filled a very special niche in St Helier: that was the Bel Sit at the top of Bath Street.

The first time I went into the Bel Sit was in the late 1970s. Giuseppe Ferri must have already been there for about ten years for he had joined Franco Miglivacca in 1969 after he left the Woodville in a big argument over the distribution of the tips. In his words, 'I said bye-bye and went down and joined Franco at the Bel Sit.' The move, as he explained it, probably sounds easier and simpler than the reality.

AMIRA delegation in Trento
(left to right) Mauro Mori, Giuseppe Bora, Bruno Zunino, Giovanni Colombo

Giovanni Colombo, Victor Cornaglia, Giuseppe Sinigaglia,
International President AMIRA

Italian Fair, Giovanni Venticinque, Giuseppe Francescon, Renzo Martin, Victor Cornaglia, 2 Musicians in dark jackets and hats

Ettore Marcoz - (if it can be sold ....)

Valerio Beltrami AMIRA International and Bruno Zunino
Photo courtesy of Jersey Evening Post

Valerio Beltrami AMIRA International and Bruno Zunino at work.
Those not working include Renzo Martin and Giovanni Venticinque
Photo courtesy of Jersey Evening Post

Victor Cornaglia showing Giuseppe Sinigalia,
International President of AMIRA how to do it properly

Still a feature in the centre of town - The old Steak House site

Inside the Steak House. Angelo Mariani's former business partner Franco Gentile on the left

60th Wedding Anniversary Franco and Pauline Morisino
Photo courtesy of Jersey Evening Post

The role of Honorary Consular Agent in the Channel Islands passes over from Renzo Martin to Serafina Jones - Venticinque
Photo courtesy of Jersey Evening Post

Maurizio Marzana, Renzo Martin, Tino Rossi at celebration lunch when Tino received the Capo di Stato
Photo courtesy of Jersey Evening Post

Mirto Sappé, Wine Merchant
Photo courtesy of Jersey Evening Post

Maurizio Marzana, Bon Viveur 2006

I went there with an Italian friend who wanted ‘a quick cup of coffee’. It was an old building and some of the furniture looked even older. The coffee machine was belching steam, which mingled with the smoke hanging in the air from countless cigarettes. The place was heaving with people, most of them Italians, standing up, as in Italy, having their quick coffee. It was a place for the them to spend some time passing the news as to who was doing what and to whom, while getting a quick caffeine fix before heading back to work.

In a sense that - and others like it - were the Italian clubs of the day, for that was the waiter’s life. They worked very hard, earned their money and got on with life. Many of them were going out with, or had married, English or Jersey girls and so, without forgetting their origins in any way, they did not need to rely on the Italian community to live a normal life. On the other hand, it was good to keep in touch. Who knows? They might hear of a better job going or learn about another opportunity that could be followed up.

As for Ferri, as he is universally known, he relished being in a position of knowing everything about the community just by keeping his ears open. He was at the hub of the Italian information exchange network.

‘Oh yes I used to know where everyone worked and how they were doing; who was leaving, who was starting. For example, Johnny Galli was a regular. He used to work at the Star, the British Hotel and the Hotel L’Horizon. When The Star closed he opened Bella Venezia on the Five Mile road. Then he had a hotel in town and when he was away on holiday out of season I used to go there and check out the property with my dog. That was just one example of being in touch with what was going on. I felt I was right there in the centre of things.’

To those who worked in a world where the customer was always right, it was a refreshing change to go to the Bel Sit. Angelo Mariani remembers one particular example of the café’s ‘customer care’; it was from the time when, with his sister and brother-in-law, he owned Gimbel’s in Colomberie, so Franco and Ferri’s Bel Sit was conveniently placed for a quick break.

‘Franco used to just stand there surveying his little kingdom; I remember a time when someone asked for a bill. He paused, tore a bit of cardboard off a box on which he could make a pretence of writing and said: ‘Sausage egg and chips, coffee, oh yes - two coffees, one bacon sandwich, that's three pounds. He threw the cardboard into the bin and then stared at the customer without another word. The three pounds, or whatever it was, changed hands pretty quickly.' Angelo said that the place had quite an atmosphere in so many meanings of the word.

The atmosphere could at times be a little intense as the Bel Sit was sometimes full of pretty drunk patrons from the two nearest pubs, the Dog and Sausage and the Soleil Levant. The food was freshly cooked but pretty basic and was not equipped with any automatic guidance system so, as a result, food sometimes by-passed the mouth and would, or so it seemed, head directly from the fork to end up on the wall. Ferri remembers that by 11 o'clock at night they used to close the doors and then let customers in one by one. 'You could see trouble coming because after an evening at the Soleil Levant and the Dog and Sausage they used to arrive in a pretty bad way and it would have been too easy for a fight to start, as we discovered on occasions.'

Meanwhile in the east of the Island Renzo Martin was progressing in his chosen career, which was proving very successful as he made the transition from head barman to manager. He was to continue his success by managing a whole group of hotels.

He was aged 27 when he got his first managerial position and thinks he must have been the youngest hotel manager in the Island. That was at Les Arches Hotel at Archirondel (now a block of flats). The hotel had the usual range of rooms one would expect but what set it apart was that it also had a very flourishing club, which featured live music from a host of stars, some who would later become very successful. Perhaps the most acclaimed was to be Engelbert Humperdinck who then was living in Jersey honing his talent under his real name of Gerry Dorsey. According to Renzo he was paid around £40 a week: 'Then he went over to London and when we asked him to come back he said he wanted £60 a week. We said no, that was too much - and then suddenly he became an international star. '

Before too long, Renzo was made general manager of the Royal Yacht at the Weighbridge as well as Les Arches and then the company bought properties in Gorey. 'In 1971 we bought the Dolphin then, the Moorings and also the Seascale.'

Renzo had become an important figure in Jersey life. I remember much later, in the 1990s, at St Martin Public Hall, I was talking to him and the then parish Constable, John Germaine. Renzo was then also the Italian consular agent, a role to which he was appointed on the retirement of Luigi Forte. I had asked John something about the future of Gorey and he replied: 'I don't know, I'm only the Connétable de St Martin, ask the Mayor of Gorey here, he's the one who knows.'

'I remember he used to call me that occasionally,' said Renzo, laughing. 'We had a good relationship with the authorities. We didn't expect anyone to like us but we did our bit as well and earned respect. It wasn't one-way-traffic; we kept our noses clean down on the pier and sorted our own problems out without the police feeling they had to always have a presence here.'

Angelo Mariani eventually came out of the army and was offered the chance of a job driving a bus in Rome: 'But, in all honesty driving a bus - in Rome! "Hell on wheels" is the English expression. But I said no, I want to go back to Jersey, so back I came, met my wife and here I am.'

He worked for a time at The Old Portelet Inn and then took on the lease at Gimbel's Restaurant in Colomberie with his sister and brother-in-law with whom he had worked at the Hotel de France. They made quite a success from a regular customer base, which included many builders: 'I remember them coming in for breakfast and lunch every day, putting their bills on tick and paying me every Friday when they had their pay packets in their hands. I trusted them and they appreciated that trust.'

Angelo's big break came when he took over the lease at the Steak House. By this time he had bought a house at Les Ametots, and also had two young children so he was risking a lot. But he needed help as the building at Charing Cross had three floors and he needed another pair of eyes to keep control. He turned to Franco Gentile with whom he had worked at the Old Portelet Inn; that had been during the time when they used to serve quite a fair few French every day. 'By that I mean that there used to be anything up to 350 as the coaches arrived every day with the French lunch trade which was massive in the Island at the time. We had a tiny hors d'oeuvres two slices of horrible salami; they call it Milano salami now, not the real thing at all, a little piece of pâté, a suspicion of salad and then gigot d'agneau for everyone.'

The French lunch trade was highly competed for by many Island establishments at the time and the prices went down and down in the rush to get cash in as the French day trippers were given their 'Tour de l'Isle' and stopped somewhere for lunch at an inclusive price. Then as now, menus could be very inventive, and that is still the case, as the current generation of diners has discovered at some places in the annual Tennerfest. Back then, I once saw advertised 'petits fritures de poisson' on a 'French lunch' menu. Fish fingers anybody?

For Angelo at least, the gamble paid off for he managed to buy the freehold of The Steak House, which he eventually rented out when he wanted to take life a bit more easily. Franco Gentile had already left by that time, having made what turned out to be a major error of judgement, in selling his share in the restaurant and raising every penny he could to establish what turned out to be the ill-fated Il Padrino in James Street.

The French day-trippers were a major source of business to the Island and not all of them relied on bus tours. Many came just for the shopping in St Helier and also looked for a reasonable meal of their own choosing. One who profited enormously from their presence was Ettore Marcoz who had been the restaurant manager at Pedro's, the restaurant owned by the Hotel de l'Europe where Mauro had started many years earlier. Ettore had bought, and then sold, a small hotel outside St Helier (the Raleigh) before buying The Mont Orgueil Restaurant in Gorey, which he owned for many years before finally selling it to the Lewis Family of the Longueville Manor. They undertook a major refit and upgrade before turning it into Suma's.

At The Mont Orgueil, Ettore was perfectly placed to trade with the French trippers who arrived on the ferry at Gorey Harbour. He would serve coffee to the early arrivals but there was a boat that docked at about 11am Jersey time and the French were already looking for lunch, as their stomachs announced it as being midday. By 1pm, therefore, he had already served a complete sitting at his restaurant before the locals and the English tourists arrived for their lunch. Returning to France at around 5.30pm Jersey time, the French trippers would have an early supper(at 6.30pm as their body-clocks were telling them) and so Ettore managed to squeeze an extra sitting in the evening before any locally based customers would arrive.

Victor Cornaglia made his big decision about Jersey two years after arriving at the Lobster Pot from the Savoy. True to its word he was approached by a representative from the Savoy after a couple of years to see if he was ready to come back to London and take over as restaurant manager at the New Berkeley in Knightsbridge. The Savoy management had told Senator Wilfred Krichefski about a possible deal and he had telephoned Victor saying on no account must he leave the Island as he was needed here.

It was not too long before Victor was approached directly; furthermore the Savoy had heard of the official reaction. 'I opened a bottle of nice champagne,' said Victor, 'and said if you were me what would you do? He said we would love you to come back but I can see your position here; you are somebody in Jersey and in your position I would probably stay. I said thank you, that is what I intend to do.'

Working closely, as was always the case, with his wife, Ida, Victor created a huge following at the Lobster Pot. He tried to buy a share of it from Frank Thomasson but negotiations stalled. Fortuitously he then heard from a friend who lived in Petit Port that the guest house next door was for sale. He purchased it immediately to ensure that he didn't lose out in any protracted negotiations and thus the Sea Crest in the west of the Island provided Victor's base for the highly successful final stage of his career right through to Ida's death and his retirement.

Victor remains based in Jersey as the Island suits him. He said that to certain Italians - Renzo, and Mirto, for example - as well as many others, the climate was better than where they come from because in that part of northern Italy they have a very harsh winter. 'We were happy and enjoyed passing on the flair with which we were brought up. People seemed to like it which is why we like the Island; it was and remains a mutual affection. We northern Italians were made very welcome. Why am I just saying the north? We were all made welcome.'

Mirto Sappé takes a similar line: 'It was a matter of fitting in and flourishing: I came from an agricultural and protestant background which was very much the Jersey heritage and, believe it or not, my patois was not too dissimilar to the Jersey equivalent. I loved the cleanliness of the place. Getting off the 'Brittany' on my very first day I looked round and thought I could get to like it here and I liked also the way people treated us when we arrived and I was struck by the efficiency of the public system.'

I asked Franco Morisino about the association between Italians and the catering trade for, during his long time in Jersey, he has had a chance to see how his countrymen had achieved so much. He had an unusual take, stressing how food is such an important part of life for all Italians.

He gave the example of holidays: 'The English look for dinner, bed and breakfast, and we look for dinner, lunch and breakfast. You go on holiday to some international destination, Tenerife for example, at twelve o'clock when everyone else is on the beach, or sleeping by the pool, the Italian visitors are queuing by the restaurant door. And being such a part of their lives, on holiday or not, we gravitate towards those jobs that complement that.'

Obviously, not every attempt to set up in business was going to succeed, but an amazing percentage seemed to have proved successful and provided the customers with what they wanted, at any level, and provided the business owners and managers with what they had been searching for when they came to Jersey all those years before. Eric Ruaro remains convinced: 'Whether it was the kitchen or dining room, when it was an Italian-run industry there was overall a better product on offer than now. The food was correct and it had flair, and was well served.'

Eric admits to turning perhaps into a grumpy old man - and why not? That is one of the plus factors about getting old. However, he said that he has made a point of visiting new places in order to see what is on offer. 'I have been to some so-called good restaurants and the food is either tasteless or good flavours are too often being hidden by over-reliance on chilli and spices so there is effectively no need for the chefs to get their basics right. The Jersey product is - except for an obvious few - losing its way, losing its charm and then we wonder why we don't get the tourists in such numbers.'

But what pushed these young Italians to succeed? The simple answer, and perhaps the obvious one, is that they became committed as many were settling down and starting a family and so they were aware of their responsibilities. But there was also another factor, as Franco Gatti recalls, it was the fear of failure.

Franco was 20 when he arrived in 1961; he found himself in a strange little island, off the map in the middle of the sea, and he carved out a life and a position for himself. 'Yes but at that age a young man leaves home to take over the world, and he can't go back having failed. You push yourself in a foreign country. It is my country now, but it was a foreign one then, and if you go home with nothing your family will say: '"what the hell have you done?" You have no choice but to succeed.'

Chapter 9

CHANGING TIMES

'O TEMPORA, O MORES.'

This memorable and much used phrase comes from the opening passage of Cicero's speech in the Roman Senate when he opened his attack on Cataline. 'Oh the times, oh the customs' is a literal translation and it is heard often in many an elaborate, if not slightly studied, expression of despair at the way customs and fashions are changing.

In a sense, it was also often heard, not in so many words, but at least implicitly, among the Italians as the dining room fashions changed and the chefs became the talked about people in the world of haute cuisine. This, coupled with the advent of plate service, signified the beginning of the end for the long reign of the maître d'hôtel. It was not a change that happened overnight; it came later in this Island than on mainland Europe, and it was certainly not accepted as inevitable by the Italian catering community in Jersey.

The late Giuseppe Francescon was running his own restaurant, Gio's, in St Helier by this time, and he had established it on traditional lines. It was his creation; he was the front man meeting and greeting while making sure the chef turned out the food that he had requested, as well as updating specialities being offered off-menu. Obviously the restaurant was too small to allow gueridon service but this was adapted to having a small moveable side table brought near the diner and so silver service was offered from that location. Just occasionally the old maître d'hôtel would be glimpsed, cooking then serving one of his memorable creations by special request, perhaps a zabaglione.

Suddenly it all became very different, he would recall, as the new fashions filtered through from the late 1970s onwards and as the new style of cuisine made its way across Europe. 'So much changed, in so little time, he said. 'It was unbelievable the way the dishes were now being prepared, for to us in the catering world it was a totally different way of cooking.'

Giuseppe used to say that he wanted to stick to the traditional approach as he had always believed that what you have on the plate is there primarily for eating. 'It has not been cooked and served for you to take a photograph. There are times when only the traditional way will suffice and I think that people will always be revisiting it on occasions.'

Giancarlo Mattioli has similar reservations about the changes as he feels something has been lost in the transition; something that was important. It was a sense of theatre and it added to the experience of dining out, but of course with the development of cuisine and the change in style and emphasis, he recognised that people these days would no longer expect that sort of service. He believes that professionalism and a whole range of front-of-house responsibilities had in a sense, been reduced: 'And the total customer experience has been lessened as a result.'

But the change was not just in food as that was merely a reflection of the change of emphasis from the dining room to the kitchen, from the maître to the chef. The range of accomplishments demanded of a senior waiter was becoming redundant as elaborately presented plate service took over.

The head waiter or restaurant owner was more than the front man meeting and greeting, Giancarlo recalled, adding that his job was to get to know the guests and know what they wanted. 'The best ones even learnt how to sum up a new customer and give them a good steer to what they were really looking for.' He would pass that over to the chef and his team in the kitchen but the chef then was second in the social hierarchy; he had to prepare what the waiter told him the customer wanted. Not anymore.'

The change now is complete, for diners no longer ask for anything special or different and are happy to be dictated to by the chef who, right from the start of this about-turn in social standing, assumed the position as the only arbiter of what could or could not be eaten and when. Some customers had great difficulty in accepting this change. I remember the late Peter Mills, the former Ryder Cup-winning golfer and proprietor of G. Orange, the St Helier wine merchants, sending a very disgruntled reply back to the kitchen when he was told by the waiter of something he had ordered: 'The chef says he does not prepare it that way, Sir.'

'My compliments to the chef,' he replied testily, 'and ask him who the hell he thinks pays his wages?'

Tino Rossi views the changes with a wry smile but his continued presence at La Capannina testifies to the continued acceptance by many that an evening out is just that; the food is a major part of the event but there is always more. He recognises that in general there has been a complete about turn, for when he started in the big brigades that moved between Switzerland and Venice, the important man who waved the flag for an establishment was the maître d'hôtel. He made sure you had a good evening and he co-ordinated the theatrical back drop to dining out. The whole experience was always more than the food on a plate.

And the other change is in the restaurant. La Capannina is known to one and all as Tino's. Were he or one of his contemporaries to have remained as the head waiter at a major hotel, the customers would have gone, for example to Tino at the Ritz, Victor in the River Room. Now that is gone, the name above the door is the chef.

There has been a big shift, perhaps even a battle as Tino put it, between the maîtres d'hôtel and the chefs. 'The maîtres were in front; they were the main point of contact with the people so, as a result, they would get all the praise and the plaudits. Meanwhile, the chef in the kitchen wasn't seen unless he was invited out to the restaurant specifically to get a compliment of one form or another.'

As Tino describes it, such were the social mores that a lot of the chefs were very shy about coming into the restaurant and there was a degree of embarrassment about the whole process. It was if those 'downstairs' were allowed, as a special concession, to come up through the green baize door. Nowadays, such embarrassment is a quaint hand-me-down from times past. As Tino commented, 'the increased use of famous chefs as a permanent feature of televised cooking programmes which, themselves, have become a branch of the entertainment industry has been remarkable. This has resulted in every chef in every restaurant wanting to become a marketable product. He wants to be a famous star beyond the kitchen.'

There are those who berate La Capannina for not following the trendy modern fashions, but Tino takes that criticism as a compliment: 'If you mean that I am being criticised for insisting on professional staff who know what they are doing and have the traditional skills and expertise, that's fine by me,' he said. 'If by being unfashionable means I have a game trolley in the season, with a selection of the best game flown in, then roast and carved in the traditional way, then so be it. If I am being criticised for serving wild salmon in season and concentrating on the food itself rather than on some way-out interpretation, then I gladly plead guilty to being unfashionable. I also gladly plead guilty to limiting the description of the dishes on the menu to what is essential rather than attempting to give a highly coloured recipe.'

'I want my restaurant staff to know how to fillet a fish, how to carve saddle of lamb or wild birds. I want them to place vegetables on a plate artistically without using their hands, and what is more important, so do my customers. I still view plate service as a downgrading of skills and a harking back to cheap and cheerful trattoria service.'

A spirited defence and one worth bearing in mind, the next time you go out and have your food dumped in front of you by a waiter who is neither sure of what is being served nor understands your question when you ask about it. At its basic level it can be seen in the simplest of matters. It may be officially frowned upon now, but asking for your warmed slices of bread to be actually toasted and therefore browner than what is being served can be quite tricky at times:

'More toast? No, you have toast, look.'

'No more toast*ed*; look it's still white.'

Ah, you want *brown toast*'… … and on it goes.

Restaurants come and inevitably, restaurants go, some very quickly. It has been said many times that those that fail go down that route from the beginning inasmuch as they do not offer the complete package. Good food is a sine qua non; however, good service and above all, from whatever source, good customer care, are all equally essential. If that were not enough there also needs to be a good business brain lurking in the background exercising proper control. Miss out on one of these and the business becomes out of balance and before too long, unsustainable.

A name can only carry so much weight on its own. A chef or a popular head waiter opening too many places becomes a brand, and in so doing will lose sight of the customers. It becomes merely a benediction from afar, to paraphrase Robin Seymour's comments earlier. Whether that benediction covers the cooking or the style of the restaurants is not enough. It will be viewed as a franchise, a pale reflection at best, of the original inspiration. So a personal presence, to a traditionalist, remains essential; for example, when Tino is away, his wife Ida will always be there keeping a family presence at La Capannina.

The change that came to the Jersey restaurant and dining scene was as a result of a shift in emphasis, a change in style. There were various attempts at chefs, excellent cooks, setting up their own places but many failed because of a lack of balance in the business coupled with a total lack of control over spending. Some have done well, perhaps not as well as their backers might like, and Jersey has also seen an attempt to trade off a famous name but that soon failed when it became very apparent that the name was there to pass over some recipes and add lustre, not to deliver the genuine goods.

Eric Ruaro reckons the Italians gave a huge boost to the creation of the Jersey independent dining out trade, away from the hotels. He said that, as a group, the Italians became dominant and that status lasted for so long because it was right for the times and the people who started were real professionals. He added that many had started in Jersey at The Star in St Helier, which had the most skilled people and 'practically all of them eventually had their own restaurants'.

'First you have to have the guts to have your own restaurant,' he continued. 'You have to have the knowledge of cooking, preparation and service to provide proper customer care and also you have to be a businessman as well. To run a restaurant profitably over a period of time is not easy but many of us, in fact it was a very high percentage of those who went down that road, succeeded.'

O tempora, O Mores: It still makes Maurizio Marzana cross to see slack service. 'I don't expect the smartest gueridon service wherever I go,' he said, 'but if you are putting a glass and a bottle on the table in front of a guest it doesn't take any longer to put it in the right place for example. It doesn't take any longer to put the spoon and fork the right way up. There are little things that anyone can get right. How often do you see other diners having to rearrange the cutlery when they sit down because it has been set wrongly?'

Preserving the best of the past by passing on skills has certainly been tried. Pietro Guglieri rose to the top as a head waiter and sommelier at the Hotel L'Horizon and then went to teach dining room skills at Jersey's catering school in Highlands College. He ran the Hotel L'Horizon dining room in conjunction with the late Giuseppe Francescon and was imbued with the same sense of professionalism and passion for the job; the two essential elements of his profession he wanted to pass on.

'I still think that Jersey people, or perhaps the British in general, do not have it their heart to wait at table,' he once told me. 'Yes they do it, many of them very well for any skill can be taught, but they don't put their heart into it, not the same as we Italians. We feel for the job, we want to look after people properly. We get pleasure looking after customers and sensing their satisfaction with what we have done but unfortunately they don't.'

The Italian heritage of cuisine and dining room skills has travelled all over the world and, according to Victor Cornaglia, is rediscovered by every generation. He says there is nothing really new in much of what he has seen.

'The Naked Chef, as he was called at the start, does all Italian dishes, the River Cafe was all Italian, Nigella Lawson is the same and they all use the very old traditional recipes. I see English chefs on television announcing a new recipe. New! My grandmother, used to do that same recipe and she taught my mother. New? No, rediscovered or even re-presented would be the most tactful, certainly the more exact, way of saying it.'

But that is not to say that the Italian restaurants in Jersey, proud as they were to serve Italian specialities, promote Italian products and the Italian way of doing things, were limited in the range of their menus. They were international, or at least western European, restaurants as one of the three musketeers, Mauro Mori, recalls.

'For example Tino at La Capannina went about things just as I did in my own restaurant,' (Mauro's of La Motte Street). 'We served a lot of Italian dishes but we also presented a lot of French standards. One of the more popular ones at my little place was duck with our own take on orange sauce and we also specialised in many different ways of presenting veal. We both offered a huge choice, changing over the years as the seasons changed, but now the fashion has changed, and not for the better. Italian restaurants now seem to be known for pizza and pasta.'

But none of these standard bearers needs to defend the food that was offered. No one who genuinely remembers what the top men provided for their customers can criticise them on that score. The continued popularity of La Capannina makes the point very effectively. Hard as it is to say (and this to Italians of all people), the truth is that many of the restaurants and traditional hotel dining rooms changed because they were becoming unfashionable. The changing zeitgeist is difficult to understand but what can be seen as the traditional way would now be judged as unattractive and out of date. That was how our parents ate. We do things differently now and we have developed our own style of self-satisfaction and arrogance combined with an unwillingness to accept any direction, advice or criticism.

Obviously, the change in Jersey was driven by external factors. International travel became a much more general way of life. Jersey Tourism's use of the phrase, 'nearer to France closer to home' as an inducement for the tourist was not going to work anymore. Travelling abroad to a far-flung location for a holiday became hardly worthy of comment. Competition between destinations was intense and the Jersey- bound tourists, as well local diners going on holiday, were being exposed to different cuisines.

People travelled farther afield and it could be the original willingness to experiment with Italian and other European food has been overtaken by a pastiche of North African and Asian food combined with a sudden desire to have chilli and strong spices with everything. To that add a touch of Tex-Mex and the result is, some might say, that over spicing of food became the norm in a certain range of restaurants with the inevitable result that, whatever else might be the result, delicate balances of taste combined with delicate (and exact) cooking are achievements that too many see as being old fashioned.

Pizza and pasta have come to epitomise Italian cooking for the masses and, contrary to Tino Rossi's memories of his formative years, the pizzaiolo had triumphed. Economics dictated that the great brigades would not be needed as plated service was easier (and cheaper) to deliver. The world where the maître d'hôtel flourished had shrunk leaving him no place to flourish, for without a brigade to run and with his role as front man and theatre director also taken away, where could he go?

Maybe that is too bleak a summary; for even if, like an honourable old soldier, the maître was destined to fade away, he wasn't going down without one last defiant and grand charge. And here in Jersey we witnessed such a spirited defence, a 'last stand' perhaps which reminded some of us, and showed the next generation, exactly what had been lost. And this last great thundering charge took place under the most mundane of banners being carried aloft: 'La cortesia non costa niente ma rende molto' it read. Courtesy costs nothing but the return is enormous.

Chapter 10

AMIRA

THE last charge of the maîtres d'hôtel: For over a century it had been the maître rather than the chef who was the defining presence of the restaurant. 'To have a famous maître d'hôtel greet you respectfully by your surname, to greet him in turn familiarly is a strong tonic for your ego,' observed Vogue in 1936.

By the 1980s, however, a revolution was underway in restaurants and hotel dining rooms. The chef was becoming the public face of dining out; it was the chef who was the star to be followed and who caught the public attention; it was in the kitchen, therefore, where the ethos of the dining establishment was now being generated. The food was created in the kitchen and the manner in which it was served became the sole prerogative of the chef and his brigade. The rule of the chef was law, not only in the way the food was cooked but as to how it was presented on the plate. Dishes were plated up in the kitchen and the waiting staff had merely to collect them at the pass and carry them directly to the table.

There was nothing new behind the philosophy of this method of working. It had always been the basis of café food, as well as that of friendly and informal brasserie and trattoria service. The change was in its elevation into the realm of fine dining and, with that, came serious implications for those who were used to the traditions and disciplines of the restaurant brigade.

Plate service signaled the end of the gueridon at each station, the end of the necessity of acquiring the presentational skills so essential to a chef de rang, the end of the cardinal task of serving food hot to the diner. Suddenly tiede (lukewarm) became an acceptable term in presentation and description, indeed there was no choice, for the plating up process and the procession of food from kitchen to table could, and often did, mean tiede at best. Apocryphal stories of young aspiring chefs (YACs) wiping the sweat from their brows before using the same hands to create the perfect picture on your plate, while the food itself was passing through the tiede stage on the way down to cold, became current and were, perhaps unfairly, believed.

As with all revolutions it started with overstatement and hyperbole to make the point. The huge cloches arriving in a convoy of waiters at the table became a source of many jokes, as overstated as the food revealed underneath them was often understated. To many diners, the nod of command from the lead waiter present, which led to the co-ordinated lifting of the cloches designed to produce the triumphal revelation of what turned out in fact to be an array of minimal portions of rapidly cooling food, became a metaphor for anti-climax. While being obvious exaggerations, these stories acknowledged the new reality and it was a reality with no place for the traditional maître and his decades of acquired skills.

The waiter's role was being reduced to basic fetch and carry. True, it was done with style and aplomb but a whole swathe of skills were now deemed unnecessary in the top dining rooms. With the demise of those skills went the status of the maître who was no longer the front man, and no longer the arbiter of what happened inside the restaurant, nor even of who would be allowed in; no longer was he the man whose name was central to the success of the establishment. The sense of theatre was largely abandoned and without a theatre no producer or director was required.

But the change was not immediate and the time that this revolution was taking place was also the time, in Jersey at least, of the greatest public flourishing of the maître's skills. Was this a conscious desire by those on the other side of the revolution to put the clock back? Probably not, but it was certainly a statement of what was being lost, a statement of skills, of flair, of style and a public affirmation that there is no 'right' way in these matters, only today's preferred way. There are, it was being said, many ways to enjoy an evening out, many factors that will make it memorable.

The agency delivering this message was the Associazione Maîtres Italiani Ristoranti e Alberghi - the association of Italian maîtres in restaurants and hotels - AMIRA. It was an international organisation with, suddenly, a very active Jersey branch led by Italo Miorin and the chosen method of getting the message across was through public demonstrations, celebrations perhaps, of members' skills at what were termed "eno-gastronomic" evenings. This description of one such event appeared in a local magazine at the time (over 30 years ago) and if the style of the article as well as the views expressed might sound familiar, then so be it.

'It was a full room, very noisy and full of Italians not that one was necessarily the cause of the other. It was noisy because the presence of the Italians resulted in 150 others coming as well. Why? Because we were celebrating and remembering; celebrating Italian cuisine and remembering the skills and the aplomb which, for a previous generation, epitomised the acme of the Italian catering experience. And let us also remember these were men who came to Jersey to run restaurants and found there was no olive oil to be had other than in a chemist for medicinal purposes. So much of what we now consider an essential part of cuisine - choices of mushrooms, of herbs, of oils, of peppers - was simply not there. These guys had to find ways of getting them. The young men who arrived in the 1950s and 1960s taught us how to eat. Without them the modern generation of aspiring young chefs so keen to pronounce on everything from bouillabaisse and borsch to birth control would simply not have had the chance to exist.

'This was the AMIRA evening; OK let's get this out of the way: "They also serve who only stand and wait." True, but this is the time when the professionals of the dining room show that there is more to serving than standing and waiting. These guys are more than waiters; they are the kings of the dining rooms. Their tool of expertise was the lamp and with that they were able to cook chosen dishes at the table and so bring a sense of excitement and theatre to eating out. It might not be fashionable any more, but who is to say that they were wrong? True the fashion may have changed, but only a puritan and a bore would say the only point of going to a restaurant was to eat.

'So in a large room surrounded by these experts in cuisine, the stage was set to appreciate an era when flair, skill and showmanship was on display next to the table and, furthermore, it was a time when foul mouthed television chefs were yet to be invented. The Italians came to the Pomme d'Or to show off their skills - not only the Jersey branch of AMIRA but their colleagues from the Isle of Capri, and from Udine in the north-east of Italy. They came with their recipes and with some genuine local ingredients to give their food that true authentic regional taste such as a dish on offer from Liguria shown by the visitors from Genova.

'So what stood out? It's difficult to say because what mattered was the whole experience, the joy of wandering around, talking to your friends and tasting, from 12 separate stations, the best of Italy and appreciating the work of gifted individuals making their own contributions to a memorable event.'

AMIRA was essentially a professional support body established in Milan in October 1955 by some 30 Italian maîtres d'hôtel. According to the official booklet of the organisation, AMIRA is primarily a social body with links to all aspects of catering including training colleges, Italian tourism and Italian Chambers of Commerce. That said, the social activities focus on traditional excellence in the dining room. AMIRA also prides itself on being strictly an apolitical professional body - not that the apolitical aspect is immediately noticeable when the conversation around the table switches to the latest political crisis back in Italy.

The booklet continues: 'AMIRA is a professional craft body and its primary function is to promote Italian culinary expertise by preserving the best of the past's traditional skills within a recognised profession which is constantly evolving to suit the taste of today's diners. The overriding philosophy behind this worthy aim was to ensure the guest received the best in terms of exceptional food and service.'

AMIRA was and remains an international body with some 40 branches in Italy as well as, in the 1980s, 14 internationally. Jersey was one of them. The organisation's motto is simple: 'La cortesia non costa niente ma rende molto' - 'courtesy costs nothing but the return is enormous'.

The Jersey branch was founded in 1978 by Italo Miorin, the maître d'hôtel at the Pomme d'Or, and he had been a member of AMIRA international since 1970. He encouraged others from the hotels, as well as restaurateurs, in Jersey's Italian community to sign up as founding members and he also received support and encouragement from the Italian Consular Agent of the time, the late Commendatore Luigi Forte and afterwards by his successor Cav. Renzo Martin. Both recognised the value in preserving this aspect of Italian heritage which, though a form of cultural osmosis, became part of our common Jersey Heritage.

From 1982 onwards, the Jersey branch of AMIRA concentrated on showcasing the best of Italian culinary skills and food, not only in Jersey but also internationally. As Italo explained; 'many of the members of AMIRA are well known. They have occupied prominent positions within Jersey's tourism industry and, as a result, they have been very active in encouraging local skills as well as promoting the Island on a grander scale.'

The chairman to succeed Italo was Maurizio Marzana and he still holds that position. 'AMIRA is an Italian association for Italians,' he said. 'We bring to the table everything we have learned through catering school in Italy as well as in our early days through to senior Italian maîtres d'hôtel.' These skills are always passed on from member to member. In essence it is the Italian way of doing things which we have always been concerned not only to protect, but also to promote.'

The chosen method of this promotion was a series of displays and tastings of food and wine, so-called eno-gastronomic evenings, both in and outside the Island. Easier to say, perhaps, than to explain, but the object was to concentrate on traditional dining room skills which the upper grade of waiting staff were expected to have and this, to most observers, meant an ability to prepare food for cooking on a lamp.

Someone going to one of the big events run by AMIRA would enter a room to find it ringed with cooking stations each managed by two of the Amirini (AMIRA members) who would be preparing and cooking a dish. This theme was repeated around the room to provide a multi-course meal, sometimes around twelve or more. Thus they could start with a selection of pastas in different sauces, continue with fish dishes, on occasions fish from the streams feeding the Italian lakes of the north, veal recipes, chicken recipes, beef dishes, desserts. Crepes Suzette or the variations, normally featured as did cheese specially flown in from Italy. Each serving station would be surrounded by the guests inhaling the aromas of the dish being prepared and marvelling at the skills on display.

The idea that somehow having your food cooked by a waiter, not a chef, was somehow second best was dismissed by Simon Walker, a well-known Jersey chef who was present at one of these events. His hobby was to collect old recipe books and he was well aware therefore that cooking is a fashion and fashions change. 'These guys specialise in certain recipes which have stood the test of time and which they have been preparing, on and off, for years,' he said to me. 'It is different and gives a huge entertainment value to an evening, but how can having your dish prepared by an expert craftsman possibly be viewed in any way as inferior?'

These events started in 1982 and ran through, more or less every other year, to 2006. They were also held in London at the Italian Trade Centre, the Palais de Congrès at Dinard and then, a few years later, back to Dinard again, but this time at the Casino. The Carlton Hotel in Bournemouth hosted a special exhibition of what Jersey could offer and also once, memorably, in Rome. There, as in all locations, the members presented and demonstrated under the Italian Flag but always, and next to it, that of Jersey.

The Tourism Department and Committee of that era were not slow to realise the positive message that was being sent out. The industry operated at so many levels that it needed to send out the message of Jersey as a centre of good food as much as it needed to concentrate on family oriented beach breaks. The Battle of Flowers was important, but so also were the waiters' races and the salon culinaire.

Jersey Tourism decided that the time had come to tell the world how the Italians had turned Jersey into a gourmet's delight. They did this by using examples. Sandro Tiboni who had been the maître at the Star Grill in the Hotel L'Horizon used to front the advertisement appearing in the UK national press which consisted of a picture of him presenting a plate of enticing food. The advertisement ran for about six months and there was a little explanation under the picture saying: 'Sandro Tiboni, Italian waiter, came to Jersey to enjoy the life and the good food. Come and join him.' It was official; the Italians in Jersey were worth shouting about.

The coverage in the press that was generated by AMIRA was extraordinary and was a free gift to Jersey. Locally, the Jersey Evening Post, while admitting privately that an assemblage of pictures of men in dinner jackets did not make compulsive viewing, also realised the strong message that was being created and broadcast by the assembled Amirini. It also acknowledged the work put in, for no financial reward and often at a personal cost, by those involved.

In the paper's report on the Dinard Casino event, the Amirini there were hailed as the Italians 'who made their careers in the Island and who now either hold senior positions in Jersey's hotels and restaurants or who have lived or continue to live in the place which has become for them just as much a home as Italy has ever been.'

But it was not just turning up to flambé something in a pan. The reporter explained that, for the Amirini, the event was a culmination of three days of solid work as they had come across to Dinard days in advance to buy, prepare and cook the stocks and all the accompaniments to the essential ingredients for the evening's entertainment.

The local French newspaper Ouest-France picked up on the event 'Quinzes maître d'hotel Italiens au casino' hailing it as an important reminder about an element of the restaurant business that had all but disappeared. A picture of Carlo Ragazzi, Mauro Mori, Tino Rossi and Italo Miorin behind their lamps appeared above a highly complimentary article and the caption under the picture read '*Servi chaud*'. Indeed servi chaud, the imperative has always been, not tiede.

The Dinard events were major excursions. Smaller but equally effective in terms of flying the Jersey Flag were the smaller trips to the Italian Trade

Centre in London and the Carlton Hotel in Bournemouth; the latter was arranged through 'connections' with the genial hotel manager there Mario Grisone. I was fortunate in being present at many of these events in my capacity as a sponsor for the wines and I remember the atmosphere of the Bournemouth trip as being on par with a school outing.

A group which included Maurizio Marzana, Italo Miorin, Paulo Crolla, Eric Ruaro and Mauro Mori piled into a minivan with containers full of cooking stock, sauce and other ingredients. We all stopped for a Sunday lunch somewhere in the New Forest which I recall included as many Yorkshire Puddings as a group three times that size could possibly have eaten - yes, Yorkshire puddings and Italians, a good mix. Then it was back into professional mode for a display of traditional restaurant skills - a shell fish dish followed by banane flambé - before a much appreciative Bournemouth audience.

The Italian Trade Centre was a much smaller affair as the Jersey team was there as invited participants by the London Branch of AMIRA. Again, promoting the name of Jersey, the small team of Italo Miorin and Victor Cornaglia prepared 'Le Delizie del Canale della Manica' a selection of scallops and mixed shellfish flambéed in brandy and wine then and then cooked in stock. At one critical moment Victor rushed off to catch up with an old friend from the Savoy and I was press-ganged to keep stirring the sauce - adding a touch more stock if necessary - until he got back. It wasn't much, but at least I can tell my grand-children I have prepared a gourmet dish in public in the centre of London.

All these activities were reported on by the international AMIRA magazine, which in one issue lauded the group's success with a picture of Mont Orgueil castle on the cover with the headline 'Jersey Tutti AMIRA'. In terms of column inches, the success of AMIRA over the years has been quite astounding and the tourism industry owes a great deal to the activities of the local Amirini.

Right from the start Italo and his committee were insistent that AMIRA would remain a non-profit organisation and the members gave their time willingly. They were happy to accept sponsorship for the wine and food but otherwise they paid out of their own pockets for what was needed. Those attending the events were invited guests and owning a ticket for one of the AMIRA evenings was something with which you could impress your friends.

Behind all this extraordinary activity was Italo Miorin who showed a pride of, and passion for, his work as well as all the traditions behind his position as maître d'hôtel. It was as if he bore the weight of Italian culinary history personally on his shoulders. He never sought any recognition for himself and, perhaps because of that, won the respect and support of his colleagues as well as the many sponsors of the events.

'Well yes,' he said to me. 'All I did was do as much as I could do. I gave my best and if it worked well that was good. But, to be honest, by myself I would have achieved nothing; it was the support I had, and it was a wonderful team.'

Italo is first to acknowledge the support of the Seymour family. 'Ok, I did a lot of the organisation and the preparation but in the end it was the support I had from the Seymour family and the Pomme d'Or Hotel that made it all possible. The Seymours really encouraged me for, without all the food preparation support from the hotel, it would have been impossible.'

One could see the look of amazement on their faces as the crowds turned up at the big events at the Pomme d'Or. It was an amazement brought about through appreciation of what was to come, not only at the size of the event but also at the range of the people there. Robin Seymour saw the whole series of events very positively: 'As far as the hotel was concerned that was a real bonus as it didn't impact on our business; indeed it was a positive image that was broadcast. It also gave our hotel employees a great deal of kudos in their own circles. Without doubt it was something quite unique and quite splendid.'

And he included his own tribute to Italo: 'You look at our maître, Italo. The time and effort he put into AMIRA was amazing, quite fantastic, but it did not have any effect on what he did for the Pomme d'Or.'

Talking to Italo, I said that the most impressive aspect of the AMIRA evenings was that there would be someone like him running around and doing everything, as it seemed, without any help. 'My God what's going to happen?' an interested observer like me would be thinking. Then suddenly everyone appeared out of the woodwork and all got their heads down and did their own thing and it just worked.

Italo, to find help in a much over-used phrase, 'followed his own dream' and as a result gave Jersey something rather special.

There came a time when it looked as if AMIRA was biting off more than it could chew and the demands on the sponsors would be too great. It was fortunate therefore that, in conjunction with the Rotary Club of Jersey, the format switched into raising money for charity. Rotary would issue and sell an agreed number of tickets so the major expenses were therefore covered with the built-in profit going to charity. As far as Rotary was concerned, these splendid evenings became the highlight of their social calendars and many prominent personalities used to make sure that their invitations were duly delivered, safely and on time.

It could be said that, as an honorary member of AMIRA, I could hardly be impartial in describing the undoubted public success of this extraordinary group of Italians, so it might be as well to quote some extracts from an account of one of the Rotary evenings written at that time by Saskia Le Monnier.

'On entering the function room at the Pomme d'Or, I was met with sensational smells of freshly prepared foods, the excited jokes of about 40 maîtres who were all having a great time while catering for 200 people and a visionary feast of stacks of seafood, local produce and flambé pans (all highly polished) in full use.

'What a treat! For anyone who has never experienced this event before, one should issue a warning. Be prepared for perfect service. Be prepared for an extravagance of Italian food, cooked to perfection, in front of you. There are no secrets; all their recipes are revealed to you, a cook's dream come true. Their ingredients were fresh produce, years of experience, and a passion for pleasing their guests. We are talking about a gathering of top Maîtres and Master Maîtres, people who have served the catering trade long enough to know how to do it properly. But the thing to watch is how they combine their experience of 'knowing how to do it properly' with a passion for their food and wine.

'The setup is quite casual. There are no tables and you are free to roam between twelve stations which each serve a different dish. These range between seafood, to homemade pasta, chicken dishes, beef dishes, fantastic sauces, vegetables, mouth watering desserts and of course coffee. The atmosphere was dominated by a sense of 'good to see you again'. All the Amarini know each other well and the Italian tie, which runs between them, is so incredibly strong it is easy to get swept away with it. I think this casual approach to catering for a big event (200 people) emphasised their experience in doing what they do best.

'The underlying feeling which became obvious during the evening was that each of the participants was proud to be there, and that they were all proud of their

cuisine; everyone was busy promoting the Italian food and wine and everyone was delighted to meet up with old friends. This was all done with such passion and gusto that it felt like an honour to be amongst then and to share their Italian ties.

'The evening of course was in aid of charity. What a way of raising money! Normally one has to go through some gruesome task to raise cash. To come to an event, as well organised as this one, to be greeted and looked after by the crème de la crème of Italian Hospitality and on top of that have to eat all that great food seems, to me, like a ticket to Heaven!'

The Rotary president, Bob Marshall, wrote to Italo in appreciation of one of the evenings: 'Cooking with lamps at the table is a dying art and the association is to be congratulated for keeping it alive.' Others wrote along the lines of 'always a treat to watch the professionals at work', and there was many a tribute along the lines of: 'It's wonderful to see an expert rolling his sleeves up and getting down to it.' My own favourite: 'It's like coming across a former champion, one of the greats, who I thought had retired, climbing back into the ring, taking on all-comers and winning.'

But as has been said, fashions change and former champions, even if they do make a return into the ring on occasions, will inevitably grow older. The concept of the maître running his brigade and preparing and assembling dishes on the gueridon is a process that would be difficult to explain to a much younger generation of diners. And, on the other side of the coin, there are no, or at least very few, young men or women coming into the profession who have aspirations to climb that particular ladder.

Nevertheless, although the Amirini might be retired, familiar faces can often be seen at a very busy evening at some local restaurant when a call for help has been answered. Suddenly old memories are kindled as that basic training and the finely honed skills are still on display.

But as I said earlier, if like an honourable old soldier, the maître was to fade away, he wasn't going down without one last defiant, history making, grand charge. And, thanks to the Amirini in Jersey we were privileged to be spectators at such an event and, in that witnessing, we were reminded of what was being lost. The AMIRA Sezione Jersey members still meet occasionally and treat themselves to excellent meals but the days of public display have gone and we are all the poorer for that. Even Italo Miorin has hung up his lamp and is no longer the fiduciario (chairman) of the local branch - that position is now filled by Maurizio Marzana. All the

Amirini can look back with enormous pride at what they achieved and the friends they made while refusing to lie down and accept the inevitable without a fight. They can look at the various honours and awards which they received and enjoy their retirement, conscious of a job well done, right to the end.

As was evident from the description of one of the eno-gastronmic evenings as seen by Saskia Le Monnier, the spirit of 'La cortesia non costa niente ma rende molto' (Courtesy costs nothing but the return is enormous) was obvious throughout all such events. But on the last such event in 2006, as the lamps were put away, we were able look back and, with the crystal clear vision supplied by hindsight, we can read quite clearly the extra line that had been added to the motto on the banner. We were never again going to experience anything similar on so grand a scale: 'Questa sera la vostra ultima esperienza.'

Taken from a Menu provided for an AMIRA evening.

Al Arrivo - *On Arrival*
Delicatezze Della Manica - *Mouth Watering Sea Bites*
Farinacei - *Pasta*
Tagliolini Tricolori - *Green and white homemade spaghetti in tomato sauce*
Selezioni di pasta di grano duro con sugi vari -
Selection of pasta in different sauces
Crostacei Pesce - *Seafood and Fish*
Delizie delle Isole Normanne - *Local scallops in our special sauce*
Filetti di pesce scelto all'acqua marina di Capri -
Selection of fish fillets Capri style
Carni - *Selected meats*
Petti di pollo all'antica - *Breast of chicken*
Bocconcini di manzo alle erbe aromatiche -
Fine strips of beef in aromatic herbs
Rognoni Trifolati alle senapi scelte - *Veal kidneys in mustard sauce*
Fantasia di Contorni - *Selection of seasonal vegetables*
Patatine Novelle - *Jersey new potatoes*
Dolci - *Desserts*
Crespelle all'arancio stregato - *Pancakes in orange and strega sauce*
Tiramisu Tradizionale - *Traditional Italian 'pick me up'*
Caffè - *Coffee*
Cioccolatini Alla Menta - *Mint Chocolate*
Un Arrivederci a Presto

Le Delizie del Canale della Manica e Isole Anglo Normane
(Delights of the English Channel and the Channel Islands)

Recipe from Italo Miorin of AMIRA Jersey Branch and presented by him and his colleagues.

500 g mixed shellfish
200 g mussels shelled and marinated for 12 hours in the classic way
1 tbsp mixed chervil, tarragon and parsley
1 clove garlic crushed on salt
2 mushrooms cut very thinly
½ carrot, ½ onion, 1 shallot cut very small or minced
2 cl Olive Oil
Knob of butter
4 cl Vecchia Romagna (brandy)
10 cl dry white wine
½ lemon
15cl Jersey cream
1 tbsp fish velouté
Salt and ground pepper

Melt the butter with the oil in high sided frying pan on a spirit lamp then add the carrots mushroom shallots and herbs. Add the shellfish and mussels to the pan and fry gently for a few minutes. Then add brandy and show a nice high flame. Add white wine and cook until almost competely reduced. Squeeze in juice of half a lemon, let it evaporate and pour in fish velouté, then bind it with cream to bring sauce to desired consistency.

During cooking give the pan the classic rotating movement to make sure everything cooks evenly.

Sprinkle with chopped parsley and then serve with whatever you wish.

(On AMIRA evenings this would be served in a vol-au-vent case, thus making it easier to eat while standing up)

Chapter 11

COMMUNITY

THE concept of community within a community is a very fashionable one and to a great extent an invention of the media whose members often use the word lazily, as a convenient shorthand; a means of pigeonholing people who might have similarities in certain respects but otherwise not much in common. Community is an easy thing to say but much more difficult to define.

Community affairs and that election cliché 'putting something back into the community' are different again but, and as regards the Italians in Jersey, the term 'community' can be used to cover such matters as engaging in activities for the common good and fitting in without making waves. But also of great importance is a generosity of spirit, combined with a genuine desire to improve matters and doing this by raising money for charity and through generous personal donations. And in considering the latter, special mention should be made of the public benefactions of Frank Berni and the charitable trust he created - but more of that story later.

Fitting in to society and sorting out their own problems became the hallmark of the Italians living in Jersey, an attitude that was highlighted at Giovanni Venticinque's 80th birthday party which was laid on by the Circolo Italiano. Mirto Sappé gave a speech in Italian - as well as in the flawless, indeed unaccented, English he had acquired over the years - explaining to the guests what the Circolo Italiano had accomplished during its existence.

He said that Circolo members made a point of supporting their own and helping those in need without going public on the matter. 'Occasionally,' he said, 'someone would arrive from Italy who tried to show us just how many extra aces he could find in the pack and then try and do things in some unacceptable manner. But we managed to persuade them to look for a job elsewhere, anywhere but here in Jersey. And they went,' he concluded.

At the time I was sitting near David Filipponi, the Bailiff's secretary, and I leaned over and said: 'Did you hear that? Your boss may not be able to get rid of undesirables, but these boys can!'

After dinner, Renzo observed to me: 'We've all had to do that to some extent. You see that in any group, any community, and I sincerely believe the Italian community here is a nice one. But what you don't want is a rotten apple in the barrel giving everyone a bad reputation. You have to get rid of it as soon as possible for a bad reputation travels very easily. It taints the whole community and can take a long time to clear.'

I reminded Renzo that Robin Seymour had said the Italians brought solid professionalism to the Island, which was a good reputation to have acquired. 'But he wasn't just talking about the stars, was he?' said Renzo. 'It was the overall level of skill and training and the ability to do a normal job well. Jersey was good for the Italians seeking a good job abroad when there was no work at home, but over the years the Italians have also paid Jersey back and as a community we have brought a lot to Jersey; it wasn't just one way traffic. You see someone like Paul Campanini and the amount he has raised for local charity over the years; it goes a long way. For example Paul has raised enough money in the last few years to buy a specially adapted car for wheelchair-confined children.

'And then there was the Italian Generosa Golf Competition. Over three years it raised over £100,000 for charity. Then we had the annual spaghetti cup that, every year, raised a few thousand. It is the sort of thing you do because you want to do it, not because you want some form of public acclaim.'

Renzo was too modest to mention the fact but the success and continuation of the last two events can be very much laid at his door.

Over the years the permit rules have gone but even before that time and with more and more Italians marrying local, or at any rate British, girls, the permanent resident Italian population grew very rapidly. 'The heights of the Italian summer population were, as I remember, around 3,000,' said Renzo, but that did not take into account their family members who would not necessarily have Italian passports. The Circolo Italiano Christmas Party shows this trend. For example there were over 300 at the 2016 party but most of those there were second generation Italian, who were neither born nor bred in Italy. The Italian sense of family has prevailed, and with that the traditions and memories of times past, but not all family members are Italian.

Any group of people sharing something common in their background will seek news and information about others in the same boat. Again I have tried to avoid overuse of the term 'community' for that implies some sort of solidity of structure with a definite division between the insiders and everyone else outside; the covered-wagons-in-a-circle syndrome. I would argue that this never really happened with the Italians in Jersey for, as Paulo Crolla told me: 'Frankly after living and working here for a few years you are bound to meet all sorts of people. They might start as customers and then they become friends. After that comes a major transition for you get invited out by them and your circle expands well beyond what others might see as an Italian community.'

What Paulo describes is a natural progression which newcomers to any society can embrace or, if so inclined, avoid or reject. The Italians, as a group, seem to have embraced it. To that you add the large number of young men from Italy, who came to Jersey and, living a normal life in the Island, naturally met young women, and so fell in love and married. There could be no sharp lines of community definition when new family ties are often created with no sense of sticking to, or being bound to, some form of national identity.

But even so, the Italians in Jersey wanted somewhere to meet up, if only for a short time, and catch up with the gossip. In the early days it might have been the Café Roma in Colomberie with Peter Guidi, who was half Italian, half Scottish, but there were others and one of the last of that family of cafés was the Bel Sit at the top of Bath Street, the domain of Ferri and Franco. As we have already heard from Ferri, it was a place where news was exchanged and, simply by keeping his ears open, Ferri was perhaps one of the best informed members of the Jersey Italians when it came to knowing who was working where and who was planning a move.

Meeting up for a coffee and a quick exchange of news was one thing but going to another level and creating an Italian Club was something that never really worked. With the success of these cafés as a social base and news exchange and, as we have discovered, the ease with which many of the Italian community integrated into society, it is hardly surprising that the clubs could not stand the test of time. If you worked long hours, if you wanted to see your wife and children when you could get away and if you could pick up the latest gossip at the Bel Sit, why bother to join a club?

Franco Gatti came up with his (not unexpected) forthright take on the transitory nature of the Italian clubs. He accepted that with all the Italians having proper home-lives here, the idea of an Italian club for exiles, as-it-were, would never really catch on and it was better to have an organisation like the Circolo of which any Italian is automatically a member. 'Also,' he continued, 'we Italians don't like clubs with rules; we are not good at that sort of thing. Look at our political history since the war. Italy doesn't do well as there are too many Italians there. To have a club you have to have rules and some respect for the rules and the committee which has to enforce them and, as a nation, we really can't be bothered with that sort of thing. The English are much better at that.'

Franco told the story of a special members' meeting of one the Italian clubs which met at an Italian owned hotel, the Chateau Valeuse, which was part of the Manzi family's business portfolio. It was that family who also owned 'Manzi's' one of London's popular and traditional fish restaurants, tucked in between Leicester Square and Chinatown. The meeting was held to elect a new club president. 'We elected the president it was Franco Gentile,' said Franco. 'When the result was announced everyone said we can't have him and then rubbished the result of the vote they had just taken.'

According to Franco, the resulting confusion and recriminations dumbfounded many of those there, not least Luigi Manzi himself: 'You Italians,' Manzi said, (and he was as Italian as a plate of pasta let me say) 'You elect a president and as soon as the result is announced and before he does anything you tell him he is no good. That's why' said Franco, 'the Italians cannot be in charge of things like clubs.'

He then added, as an afterthought: 'Maybe they shouldn't be allowed to run countries either.'

Giovanni Venticinque and others certainly tried to make the idea work on more than one occasion but they didn't succeed and it was the much looser organisation of the Circolo Italiano, which automatically included everyone Italian born, or of Italian descent, that proved to have the staying power. It remains to this day as a type of focal point for the community in the loosest sense, as well as being a good source of communication to and from the consular agent of the time.

Eric Ruaro had a very individual take on the apparent ease with which the Italians in Jersey seemed to integrate so easily. In his view the community, if it could be called that, was never inward looking and of course many at that time married local girls. He has a theory that because

Italy is a relatively new nation state - in 1848 it was written off by Metternich as 'a geographical expression' - the regions have had to co-exist with their different identities and so a habit of muddling along together is long established.

'The Italians seem to integrate well wherever they go,' he said. 'Don't forget we are a young country and as Italians, rather than Piedmontese, Sicilians or whatever, we are about a century-and-a-half old. The country was a group of some twenty different regions, twenty different ways of living, twenty different dialects, and twenty different ways of cooking. So we had many years of practice at adapting to neighbours who were different in many ways.'

It was not long before the Tourism Committee woke up to the fact that with the success of the Italians in the catering business came readymade copy for press releases and advertisements. We already learnt how Sandro Tiboni, the maître at the Star Grill at Hotel L'Horizon, was the subject of an advertisement encouraging people to come to Jersey to enjoy the good food available. The official Jersey public line was to adopt the Italians as part of the community and they could then be pictured as an essential part of Jersey which contributed to making the Island worth visiting. It was, as some would see it, part of ultimate acceptance into the Jersey community and a sign of successful integration.

The Italians were by now flexing their muscles in public and the first dramatic evidence of this was the creation of the Italian Food Fair in Halkett Place. There are now many variants of this event with a variety of national themes, but this was the first of them and it distinguished itself from many others in that it was not launched as a commercial event, but as a way of showing off what could be achieved. It was an invitation to the whole Island to come and enjoy the Italian culinary creation in Jersey and in saying that, the word 'invitation' is used wisely in this context inasmuch as, for the first year, Italian week was free.

Whoever came could enjoy small helpings of pasta from the various stalls with a variety of sauces, or other Italian specialities, without paying. Small tasting glasses of some wines were free but a charge was soon imposed to prevent the inevitable abuse of hospitality by some who saw the occasion as a way of being paid to get drunk.

In effect, for a few days Halkett Place became Piazza Halketta and in the few years of its life it was augmented by folkloric bands, displays of Italian icons such as Ferraris and Alfa Romeos and for a few days a short stretch of Halkett Place between Minden Place and Beresford Street was closed. It was never going to be a permanent feature of the annual calendar because of its nature of being a shop window for the community. The free nature of the event was changed as small charges were levied to cover costs but it was never designed as anything other than a demonstration of 'who we were', it was not, nor was it ever meant to be, a money-making event. Somewhere to have fun; somewhere perhaps to dance - I remember my wife dancing the foxtrot with Ettore Marcos, owner of the Mont Orgueil Restaurant - somewhere to meet your friends. But gradually the costs mounted - particularly from official sources - and the decision was made to leave it as it was in people's memory, rather than move location and change into a major commercial event.

The Tourist Magazine, 'Taste of Jersey' hailed it as 'Jersey's little Italy' where the visitor could 'see the food, not only pizza and pasta, but wine and culture from one of Europe's great gastronomic countries. All with an Italian band serenading al fresco diners every lunch time between 11 and 4 from Monday to Saturday.'

In May 1988, the Jersey Evening Post reported on the second year of the Italian Food Fair in Halkett Place: *'Anyone in the vicinity mid-morning (yesterday) could not have failed to notice the Continental atmosphere as a procession of carriages and Italian vehicles made their way to where the Fair had been set up.*

'In the carriages were the Constable of St Helier, Mr Fred Clarke and Mrs Clarke, Tourism president Senator John Rothwell and the Italian Consul (sic) Mr Renzo Martin.

'Also in the parade were an Italian three-piece band, La Cucina, and a host of pretty girls from the local Italian community who set the festive mood dancing to the lively sounds.

'This is the second Italian Food Fair to be held and, according to Mr Martin, who is chairman of the committee which stages the event, it is more colourful and professional than the first.

'As he told the JEP, next year there are plans to bring an Italian opera singer to the Island as part of the celebrations.

'In his view it is better to build the fair up gradually and learn from experience, rather than making it too big too quickly.'

This was the first of the national fairs which are now a feature of Jersey life. Being in Halkett Place it centred around the three Italian restaurants which were there, La Capannina, Pizza Express and Gio's. Obviously other restaurants joined in but generosity can only be extended for a limited time and in the face of the rise of the inevitable freeloaders taking advantage of what was on offer, the community lost heart and did not want to throw their money at those freeloaders and so the idea died.

But not totally, for by that time the Portuguese community decided to do something similar and they held their first festival in Cattle Street using a similar formula but, good as it was, charging enough to cover costs with a little over, gave it a different feel. That said, the fact that it has been a continued success over the years shows that the commercial formula they employ has been the right one for continuity. However, nothing before or since has been able to capture the spirit of those first couple of years of the Italian food Fair in Halkett Place.

Meanwhile that other great showcase of Island cooking, the annual Salon Culinaire, was an annual feature of the season and the Island's chefs relished their chance to be over the top and a bit dramatic in presentation. The Town Hall became swamped with prepared meats in chaud-froid sauce towering over the visitors, and fish surrounded by intricate patterns of canapés and small temptations in aspic. The chefs were encouraged to enter by management in the hope their hotel would gain valuable publicity.

John Wileman recalls: 'For the most part, my staff was Italian, always first class and artistic. Chef Pietro Alzetta won top awards for year after year in the Annual Salon Culinaire. Eventually the president of Tourism, Clarrie Du Pré, begged me to stop entering Chef Alzetta's exhibits. He argued that I was being unfair to other hotels by entering Alzetta year after year. Naturally I refused and Alzetta continued.'

Renzo, as we know had become a very successful manager of a group of hotels, but how did he also become the Consular Agent when the previous holder of the office decided to retire? 'Basically I was approached, he answered. 'Luigi Forte had been asked to put forward a few names and he came to me and said he was planning to include my name on the list.'

At the time that Renzo took over the consular agent duties, issuing passports for Italians resident in the Channel Islands was one of his tasks but that stopped with the introduction of digital and biometric passports that were impossible to produce locally. EEC and the EU rules keep on changing and there is always, according to Renzo, problems to deal with, such as trying to help with Italian-based pension problems. 'Being an Italian Government official, albeit unpaid, there were always types of forms and issues to be sorted out which I might not have had the power to do personally, but I could still make sure that the problem went to the right place where it could be solved.

'Passports still have to be renewed and the documentation prepared; it's just that the final process cannot happen here. You have to go to London much more often now, but it is not a hard job, although very detailed on occasions, and you get to meet everybody, which is always a bonus. But nevertheless I sometimes wonder how I managed to fit it all into my life for it was no picnic running the five hotels in the group.'

'One thing for which I was very grateful was that the Consul General and the Ambassador both came to Jersey. It was the first time the Ambassador had ever come here and it was a great honour for me to be the official showing him around and meeting all the elected officials and dignitaries of Jersey in their official capacity.'

Thirty eight years in the role and Renzo has now stepped aside in favour of Serafina Jones-Venticinque, the daughter of Giovanni Venticinque and his wife Maria. She arrived in Jersey as a very small baby and one of her first decisions over five decades later was to back the creation of an Italian Cultural Festival 'Viva Italia' due to be held in May 2017. Its success has yet to be analysed but one obvious move, which can only be applauded, is the number of second generation Italians who have emerged, as local residents, to help celebrate their own roots. Familiar names such as Marzana and Calvani are shown to be members of the organising committee; Giorgina Marzana (Maurizio's daughter) and Marcus Calvani, (the son of Giuseppe Calvani of La Buca and now La Cantina) are among those who have stepped forward.

But no consideration of the Italian community's role in - and contribution to - the Island of Jersey can be complete without mention of the head of one family who came here not to work, but to retire at the end of a very successful career, Mr Frank Berni. He was an Italian with a great spirit of patriotism and sense of national identity who, in 1969, came to live in Jersey. Together with his brothers Aldo and Marco, he had created in the UK the phenomenally successful chain of restaurants, 'Berni Inns'.

The Berni brothers modelled the chain on restaurants they had seen in America. They introduced the post-war British public to its own home-grown restaurant chain, which came with its own pre-stylised restaurants with Tudor-looking false oak beams and white walls. The first Berni Inn opened on 27 July 1956 at *The Rummer*, an historic pub in the centre of Bristol. The chain offered slick service and value for money, achieved partly by offering only a limited meat-based menu and a relatively small wine list. It had a loyal and regular following and quickly expanded through the 1960s, first throughout Bristol, and then through much of the rest of the country although in Bristol, certainly to the student population of the 1960s, the chain was known as much for its popularisation of the schooner of sherry in its accompanying sherry bars as for the steaks upstairs. The company went public in 1962.

A typical menu was: - starter: melon boat with maraschino cherry, or prawn cocktail. Main course: steak, gammon steak or plaice with chips, and peas. Dessert: Black Forest gateau or a choice from the cheese board (Danish Blue, Stilton or Cheddar) and then Irish coffee and After Eight mints. At the top of the range as the chain started, a prawn cocktail and fillet steak or scampi combination cost less than a pound. Schooners of sherry were the favoured apèritif, and all this was served to customers installed at deep red velour banquettes. The most frequently ordered meal, even as late as the 1980s, was prawn cocktail, steak and Black Forest gateau. This is sometimes called the Great British Meal. Yet it could be argued that, cooked well and served as it should be, with good ingredients, this often ridiculed dinner can still be turned into something special.

The wine list, like the menu, was equally cleverly designed for a market which was not used to dining out and so was geared to those who were unwilling to look foolish in front of their family or friends by getting lost in pronunciation of strange drinks or confused by menu French. For example, the small list included Bulls Blood, Blue Nun and others which were essentially English names and therefore easy to read.

After Frank decided to retire to Jersey, the business was sold in 1970 for £14.5 million to Grand Metropolitan, which later absorbed its own Schooner Inns into the Berni brand. In 1990, the chain was sold to Whitbread, which re-named it 'Beefeater Pubs'.

Frank Berni was born in his ancestral village of Bardi in the Apennines on 30 October 1903. He remained in Italy until his education was completed, before setting off to join his father's business in Wales in the early 1920s. The Berni family had once run a menagerie in Paris, but the story goes that the animals were eaten during the siege of Paris during the Franco Prussian War of 1870. Frank's grandfather set off to find new fortune in the prosperous mining valleys of South Wales, where he built up a chain of cafés known as 'temperance bars'.

When Frank Berni arrived in Jersey in 1969 he was a very successful man; the Bernis, with the Fortes, were the two best known and perhaps most successful Italian catering families. Mr Berni was a man of great generosity, and he loved to help people, especially Italians who had fallen on hard times. With some 3,000 Italians in Jersey at that time, there was always someone who faced some special and unforeseen need so there was always someone who could be helped back on his or her feet.

The consular agent in those days was Luigi Forte, who was, as a cousin of Charles Forte, known to Frank Berni and together they were able to make sure that Mr Berni's generosity was appropriately targeted.

Then in 1976 the Terremoto del Friuli, the Friuli Earthquake, shook the region in early May. Up to 978 people were killed, 2,400 were injured, and 157,000 were left homeless.

In response to the earthquake the Italian community was represented by the newly-created Circolo Italiano and set out to raise money to help those in need in Italy; the Circolo, by it all inclusive nature, could represent the whole community in this effort. Giovanni Venticinque, who served in the army near to the epicentre, remembers well the first big community involvement by the Circolo.

When that earthquake in Friuli struck, those from the region, including Giovanni Venticinque, his wife Maria, Tino Rossi from La Capannina, Giovanni Fassetta, who for many years was a feature of the St Helier market with his Italian delicatessen, were among the early Italians who came together with the desire to help. There was also Giovanni Galli from the Rosebank Hotel and others including Mario Dugini, who was for many years the manager at the Atlantic Hotel.

'We set out to help,' recalls Giovanni Venticinque, 'and do what we could. An English friend who had a caravan company in London let us have a vehicle at a very reasonable price and, with the money we had raised, decided to bring this caravan full of blankets and clothes to Udine in the north near the Yugoslav border, the nearest big town to the disaster.

Despite a crash on the way, we got there and we had a wonderful reception from the local minister for the regional disaster response. We were even given a special helicopter view of the disaster site and were shown how our contribution could help. In its own way it was a memorable time.'

The formation of the Circolo allowed the money which used to be given by Frank Berni to Luigi Forte to assist the needy in the Italian community to be transferred to the Circolo Italiano, so that it could take over the task of distribution. It was also Frank Berni's wish that the Circolo would organise a Christmas party for the Italian children. The event became so popular, that not only the children, but also the rest of the family began to take part, and that is the Christmas party that still takes place every year and is almost always oversubscribed.

Mirto Sappé had never joined any of the original Italian clubs for, as he says, he was working too hard to belong to anything. 'Working every hour of the day and with four children by the time I was 28, my life totally revolved around my job and my family. However you belonged to the Circolo automatically by virtue of being Italian or having very strong Italian connections in some way. Second or even third generation Italians, if they have a link to Italy, can come along to our events. However, I never really got involved until the Italian weeks which started back in the 1980s.

'The Circolo looks after the community,' he said. 'When necessary it helps raise money for disaster relief in Italy as it does at the moment with the series of earthquakes in Central Italy. Indeed the tragedy in the Friuli back in 1976 was one of the great drivers of establishing a successful Circolo and the role of the Berni Family and later the Berni Trust cannot be overestimated.'

Jurat Geoffrey Grime met Frank Berni soon after he arrived in Jersey. Geoffrey was a young and newly qualified accountant and Frank was a retired successful businessman, already a pensioner. They came from totally different worlds yet struck up an immediate rapport based on the good relationship that should exist between a client and a professional adviser. Geoffrey had immense respect for Frank's business acumen and would suggest on many occasions that he wrote a book on business and management. 'Had he done this I am sure it would now be a text used at business schools.' he said.

He remembers frequent meetings in the early days as Frank was getting his affairs in order in his new Island home. Monthly lunches at Mauro's in La Motte Street became a feature of their relationship and they would always pay for lunch on an alternate basis. Geoffrey recalls that Frank paid for the first lunch and he paid for the second; he was nervous hosting a man who knew more about wine and food than he ever would. 'I suggested he ordered and he refused saying I was the host. Any wine you like will do, he said, as long as it is Italian.'

'The wine I chose could not have been a good one,' said Geoffrey. 'When I got home the next day there were six cases of Italian wine on my doorstep together with a copy of Hugh Johnson's World Atlas of Wine.'

The story, according to Geoffrey, shows Franks humour as well as his generosity. Over the years he has been very generous to his close and distant family as well as many charities and good causes.

'His charity did not stop in Jersey,' said Geoffrey. 'My wife and I, at Frank's suggestion, once visited his home town Bardi. Being shown round, I could see the very visible results of his good works including the Infants' school, a home for the elderly and the refurbishment of the church bells; I am sure there were many more examples and not just in Bardi.'

Indeed there were, not only in Bardi but also in the United Kingdom, in Jersey and of course in Italy. As a general rule, according to Geoffrey, Frank Berni did not like to have his name in big letters attached to any of his charitable grants: 'He gave money because he wanted to, not to make a public display.' Nevertheless here in Jersey his name will forever be associated with the Berni Gallery in the Arts Centre and of course the Berni Hall, the community space behind the Catholic Church in St Martin, only a stone's throw from the Catholic cemetery where he was buried on 14 July 2000.

Chapter 12

ACHIEVEMENTS AND AWARDS

IT was around the turn of the century that some of the Italians whose careers had been a feature of Jersey for many years were becoming something of interest to the media in terms of their age and experience.

Awareness of what they had achieved personally and the importance of their legacy to the Island were slight. With the focus on what is happening at any given moment and with a large number of young men and women starting out on their careers, the corporate memory of a news room covers a very short span. Nevertheless there was a feeling that the older Italians had achieved something long ago and there was a dim understanding that there was more to Italian food than pizza and pasta, so older reporters and presenters were instructed to produce something to reflect those days that perhaps their listeners and readers remembered.

Thus it was that the Italian legacy in Jersey began to make the news pages.

'In the late 1940s, a 15-year- old Italian boy left school and started his first job in the hospitality industry, as a bell boy, a lift boy, in one of San Remo's top hotels. 61 years later in Jersey, his long career was recognised. Members of AMIRA (the association of Italian restaurateurs and head waiters) gathered to celebrate the career of Bruno Zunino, one of the proprietors of La Taverne Restaurant in St Helier. Hamish Marett-Crosby was there and produced this commentary on events as they happened.

'"Imagine you are approaching the end of your career; indeed it has continued well past what is seen as the natural stopping point. Imagine also that you have made a success of your chosen profession in which you have many colleagues who have remained friends even if they are all your competitors. Yet, despite being in competition, you discover that they are going to honour you with an award to celebrate your many years at work. By the way, the word 'many' is well chosen for so far, your career has spanned 61 years and still counting.'

"A little thought put out there to set the scene for the members of the Jersey branch of AMIRA, the association of Italian maîtres d'hôtel and restaurateurs, as they gathered to honour their colleague Bruno Zunino by presenting him with the sash of Ordine Grandi Maestri della Ristorazione - a Grand Master restaurateur."'

Those last three paragraphs were the introduction to a report on BBC Radio Jersey back in April 2012 when the station reported on a cause for celebration amongst the Jersey Italians in the catering industry.

Some of us look forward to retirement, some dread it, and there are some who never retire but continue to work because they are doing something they love. Whatever statement might reflect one's own situation, it is worth looking back on your life at work and considering, how would you remember it. How would you have liked to remember it and how would your friend and colleagues view it? Is there in fact any better form of acknowledgement of a job well done than an award given by your peers, those who really know what it is you do and how you do it? Put those two concepts together and you get a gathering of Italians to celebrate the career of one of their own.

There has always been a permanent sense of commitment within Jersey's Italian community to promoting its national catering traditions and it remains a powerful force. Evidence of this can be seen on a regular basis and a recent example has been the bestowing of the title *Grand Maestro della Ristorazione* to Bruno Zunino of La Taverne Restaurant. He joined an impressive list which included Vittorio Cornaglia, formerly of the Savoy Hotel River Room, the Lobster Pot and the Sea Crest, the late Giuseppe Francescon of Hotel L'Horizon and Gio's, Maurizio Marzana of the Grand Hotel and Bon Viveur, Valentino (Tino) Rossi of La Capannina and Italo Miorin, maître at the Pomme d'Or and for many years the chairman of AMIRA.

The chairman of AMIRA, then as now, was Maurizio Marzana who said that there was no better person than Bruno Zunino to receive such an award as he had been working for over 62 years in the business. 'It is a great person to whom such an honour can be given,' he said. 'Our members are still working and, as we know, Bruno is very active in his business. So it is great to recognise such a person who still has the heart and the will to carry on working even if he is well past the time of the usual retirement age.'

Of course the reasons for anyone to carry on working well past retirement age are many and varied but for a popular restaurateur, work and the enjoyment of connections right across society are inextricably linked. Work keeps a man in his restaurant but everyone comes to visit him there. It becomes an essential part of life without which a man could well wither away from lack of social nourishment.

To have your abilities recognised by your peers is a great accomplishment, but recognition of years of hard work by one's family is also important, particularly as being a restaurateur means anti-social hours and the first to feel the effect of those are the nearest and dearest. Bruno's son Peter Zunino did not follow his father into the catering profession but, as he admits, he was imbued with its values from an early age. In a sense he was so deeply immersed, albeit vicariously, in the catering trade that so much of what goes on is second nature in a way: 'I am so delighted that my Dad's hard work and his dedication to doing things properly, the way things should be done, has been recognised today,' he said at the time.

Peter said that he saw the award as a reminder that there is more to a restaurant than the work in the kitchen. Like many, he believes implicitly that a good restaurateur is there to make sure that everyone's evening is memorable in more ways than the presentation of the food on the plate. He said he had been taught from a young age that there should be a sense of occasion, sometimes even theatre, to make somebody's evening out that bit special. He felt that the growing cult of the celebrity chefs meant that these days their activities were presented as the be-all and end-all of dining out: 'So,' Peter continued, 'I am glad for my Dad on a personal level but I am also glad to see traditional restaurateurs like him keeping silver service and other traditional front of house skills alive. I think that's very special.'

The Grand Master's sash was presented by the chancellor of the order, *Cancelliere Ordine Grandi Maestri della Ristorazione* Valerio Beltrami, who had flown in to Jersey from near Lake Maggiore in the foothills of the Alps in north western Italy. He told those at the celebration that he saw it as important to reinforce connections between AMIRA members across Europe and not just at their conventions in Italy. He also said that he understood that AMIRA reflected the post-war origins of Jersey's hospitality industry which had been to a large extent, if not Italian owned, certainly Italian managed and run.

Bruno himself we have met before in these pages and despite working for so long, joked that if he could make his toll of working years hit 75 he might then consider taking early retirement. He also acknowledged the rumour that when the final day comes and he was called by the great maître in the sky, he wanted his ashes put in the restaurant so his presence would continue to be felt: 'I have decided that I will have the urn put on a shelf near the steps in the restaurant so that I can keep a good eye on things and make sure the money is spent wisely,' he said.

Bruno's award came from the association of his peers but there are also awards from the State. Of course anyone growing up in Britain is used to our own system of medals and civic awards; after all, twice a year we hear that local people have been honoured for what they have achieved. Foreign awards are less easy to understand. So when we heard, back in June 2013, that the owner of La Capannina Restaurant in Halkett Place, Tino Rossi, was awarded the Capo di Stato (literally, 'head of state'), we asked ourselves 'what could this mean'?

The day after the presentation, a picture of Renzo Martin, then the Italian consular agent in Jersey, Maurizio Marzana the chairman of AMIRA and Tino himself holding the award was published in the Jersey Evening Post. Under the picture was a report by Lucy Stephenson on the celebratory lunch following the award ceremony at La Capannina which carried the headline 'Award for man who helped shape Jersey's dining culture.' In the article she explained that the medal, presented by the Italian Government is awarded to people who have reached the top of their profession and stayed there for many years.

'It has a similar status to the UK's MBE,' she wrote. 'Mr Rossi was nominated for the accolade by the Jersey Branch of the international Italian catering association, AMIRA.'

'Speaking after the event to honour his award, Mr Rossi, who is married and has two children and one grandchild, said he was one of the last Italian restaurateurs who moved to Jersey after the Second World War, still working.'

'They are all retired now,' Tino told the JEP. 'I am the only one left who carries on working. I like it and I love it and I love my customers. I would like to carry on for a few more years.'

'The award is a great honour that I never expected. It is great, and especially so coming from the Italy's Head of State.'

Renzo Martin, who presented the award on behalf of the Italian Government, said that Tino and others like him who moved to the Island in the 1950s had played an important part in helping to shape Jersey's restaurant culture. 'He has done so much for the Island,' he went on to say. 'People like him are the original restaurateurs, of traditional food, obviously. Tino has been here in Jersey over 50 years and this restaurant is still renowned as one of the best in the Channel Islands.'

Speaking at the time to BBC Radio Jersey, Maurizio Marzana described Tino as an outstanding maître and as he had been at the top of his profession for so many years and he was undoubtedly an excellent recipient of the award. The process was started by AMIRA in Italy. That organisation made an official approach to the Italian government with their recommendation for this very prestigious award. He stressed that this award was not handed out every year on some arcane rota system: 'It is definitely a one-off and a very special honour for Tino.'

The same point was taken up by Renzo Martin who said this was the first such occasion in Jersey and it was a great credit to Tino for being selected. 'Here he is in Jersey still in the industry and he has also done so much for AMIRA for so many years. We should also thank the Jersey people for supporting him for so long. I know there are many new restaurants always opening up promoting whatever new style is in vogue but this is the one, the best one of course, that still serves traditional food.'

Tino, give him his due, was looking more than a touch embarrassed to be exposed to this shower of public compliments but he had this to say when approached by a well wisher who had been coming to La Capannina since shortly after it opened and who congratulated him on his success and staying business, saying it was an extraordinary achievement.

'Yes it's been a long road,' he said, 'and I have just been plodding along year after year and I can hardly believe that I am still here, still working very hard and still trying to achieve whatever is possible. All those years ago, for example, olive oil used to be only available in the chemist. Markets change and transport gets more efficient and at that time, do not forget, the influences in catering were predominantly French, but we managed to make an impact and introduce little Italian specialities for you all to enjoy.'

Tino is also a *Grand Maestro della Ristorazione*, one of the six so honoured in Jersey by AMIRA and his restaurant also had the distinction of being graded in 1989 as a 'Cravattino d'Oro' one of very few outside Italy, which was awarded by AMIRA International. The name comes from the little pin in the shape of a golden bow tie, the logo of the AMIRA, and the International Association's web site shows only three such awards outside Italy. It seems remarkably few, so all credit to Tino and his long stint in Halkett Place.

It was a few years after the award of Tino's Cravattino d'Oro that my wife and I were in Verona. We were dining at the Ristorante Marconi just off the Piazza della Erbe and the maître serving us was wearing his AMIRA membership pin. He seemed to understand, and speak, basic English and, as we were a bit early and he was not busy, I congratulated him on being an Amarino and pointed out that, strange as it might sound, I was also a member, albeit an honorary one.

Miraculously, his English suddenly became much better and the conversation flowed as he sought more details as to why I had been so honoured. Then he asked the question 'which branch?' 'Jersey,' I replied. 'Jersey,' he mused, 'Jersey,' he said again, as he tried to place why he had heard of the Island. While this little play continued, I was reflecting on the Island's tabloid image and was expecting some comment about a mafia money haven, or something along those lines. Meanwhile he was trying to work out why Jersey rang a bell. 'Jersey,' he continued, 'Jersey,' he said again in triumph, as his memory finally made the connection, 'Si, Jersey, La Capannina; Tino Rossi!'

'Fair enough,' I remarked, to my wife. 'If, coming from Jersey, we are going to be known for one thing while in Verona, La Capannina will be as good as, if not better than, most other options.'

There are of course awards from your peers, as in some of the AMIRA - sponsored events but also awards from the Italian State. Of these there are examples in Jersey of the Stella Del Merito del Lavoro, one of the local recipients of which was Giovanni Venticinque on 4 June 1996. Is there an English equivalent? Perhaps a BEM could be an approximate guide.

According to the offical explanation, this is awarded to 'Italian workers outside of Italy who have given proof of exemplary patriotism, of hard work and integrity, resulting from separate attestation of diplomatic mission or consular office.' It can be granted to workers who have provided service continuously for a minimum period of 25 years and is reserved therefore for those over a minimum age of 50 years.

The official citation, in translation, for Giovanni reads: 'Mr Venticinque arrived in Jersey in 1956 and is an example of a typical figure who emigrated from Italy who, from the position of head chef, knew how to progress through the ranks of the hospitality industry to become general hotel manager, thus giving a fantastic example of the commitment and professionalism required of the Italian vocation in the hospitality industry.'

Nine years later Giovanni was created Cavaliere of the Order of Merit of the Italian Republic, one of the highest Italian decorations. The paragraph, which appeared in an Italian newspaper, quoting the official citation, stated: 'G Venticinque is an example of national pride, that thanks to his intelligence and his willingness he made headway in his chosen career in the island of Jersey. He became a hotel manager and also president of the 'Circolo Italiano' Jersey. His professionalism and help to the immigrant workers abroad has helped our nation progress on the Island of Jersey.'

Another prominent Jersey Italian who became a recipient of a State award was Maurizio Marzana, who moved to Jersey for a couple of years to learn English and so improve his prospects. He arrived at a time when the Italians dominated the Island's catering industry. Forty-four years later (and, by the way, speaking fluent English) he is still here and earlier this year travelled to a ceremony at the Italian Embassy in London to receive the Stella di Merito del Lavoro (Star of Merit for Work).

Officially the Ordine al Merito del Lavoro, Order of Merit for Labour, is described as "an organisation for those who have worked with skilfulness, contributing to the development of the nation and to a better status to the workers and is awarded to Italian nationals, wherever they live and work, for their achievements in the whole range of professions and areas of commerce.' As part of his nomination Maurizio was recognised for his work as chairman of the Jersey Branch of AMIRA.

And if ever the point were to be made about young men coming to Jersey fully trained, Maurizio is a good example. But he is also just one example among many of how Jersey benefitted from the Italian catering culture that provided a fully trained staff arriving as if by magic and able to communicate to the customers, without the hotel management having to be over-concerned, or involved, in the recruitment process.

Married to Sally with two children, Maurizio's career has moved away from smart hotels and large dining room banqueting suites. For over 25 years, he has been a joint owner of the Bon Viveur, the small hotel/guest house and very busy informal restaurant in St Aubin: 'It's our own business, my partner Enzo and I were responsible to no one else, except of course our families. It may not be as grand as the dining rooms and restaurants of my youth,' he said, 'but running your own business is a powerful attraction and very rewarding.'

Another man who has been acknowledged by the Italian Government for his work in Jersey, albeit in a different forum, is Renzo Martin. Succeeding the late Commendatore Luigi Forte as honorary Italian consular agent for the Channel Islands, Renzo was in 1992 himself decorated as a *Cavaliere*, a knight of an Italian order of chivalry and one of the honours of the Italian Republic which are given by the president after accepting advice.

Looking back on his life in Jersey, Renzo has come a very long way from his arrival at the Corona Hotel with Setti Pozzi. By any standards, he has achieved a great deal. He was managing director of a hotel group consisting of five hotels. Somehow he managed to combine that with being consular agent, an active member of Rotary, a member of the IoD and captain of the Royal Jersey Golf Club. Finally, he has been instrumental in raising many thousands of pounds for charity. As the world judges these things, he has been very successful as a result of his move to Jersey.

Renzo looks back at his achievements quite dispassionately. 'Yes, it has been a privilege and very interesting but I never forgot it was the Italian consular agent who was invited to all these events, not Renzo Martin. It was the agent who was asked to attend at Royal Visits, to come to celebration of Royal Visit dinners and all those other events, not me. It is always important to remember that. However, it is nice that the position you hold is recognised. Of course I look back with personal pleasure that I have been privileged to meet the Queen, to have been to a Royal Garden Party and had tea at the palace. I am grateful to have been included with the ambassador and the consul general in all the occasions surrounding their visit to Jersey.

'Equally, as captain of Royal Jersey Golf Club, I got invited to all manner of events, which was also a privilege but you must never forget that the position is what makes it. It is only coincidental to that situation that you are involved.'

In essence, Renzo's advice is very sound and should be remembered by many, especially in the media, or in any occupation that obliges people, as part of their job, to associate with the rich and famous. Keep your head and remember that you are a conduit at best, perhaps even cannon fodder, not the main guest of the event. Do no forget that salient fact, otherwise madness beckons.

Individual achievements abound within the Italian community: Victor Cornaglia, for example represented Britain at the Rencontre Gastronomique de Genève in 1974, which is an extraordinary achievement. Others achieved special mention in the national press and not only that of the United Kingdom. Mauro Mori for example was recommended as one to look out for by the influential French paper, Le Figaro. Giuseppe Francescon achieved the status of being the United Kingdom Headwaiter of the Year back in 1989, the year he was also presented to the Queen. Meanwhile Tino Rossi, defying his age as he worked past the time most of us are long retired, celebrated 50 years and a host of mentions and awards at La Capannina.

According to Mauro, being given awards was not the reason for doing what they were did while achieving so much on a personal level, it was a bonus. 'We all loved the job we were doing, no matter how hard we worked. It was a part of our lives.'

Crucially, as has already been stressed, Mauro and his colleagues brought with them the discipline and skills of the brigade and the experience of those brigades in some of the best hotels in Europe. Thus, when I started writing this book I seriously considered using as a title the famous Julius Caesar line; *'Veni, Vidi, Vici'* (I came, I saw, I conquered). I saw this as a reflection, not in terms of their public achievements, but in the personal accomplishments of the Jersey Italians in leaving behind a country that was struggling economically and setting out to make a good living, to succeed in their chosen profession, for they certainly did regard what they were doing as a profession. It was also a passport, for many of them, to achieve success and, as we have seen in just a few examples, to be recognised by their peers and by their country for their achievement.

Chapter 13

AVE ATQUE VALE

THOSE Italians who have stayed in Jersey have spent a much greater part of their lives in the Island than they have ever spent in Italy. Many left their own country in their teens or early twenties and those of that generation are now mostly well into their seventies, if not beyond. However, many of them have the means to go back to Italy if they so wished, but they are conscious of the ties they have built in a place where they have been fortunate to have achieved so much.

Looking back over nearly 60 years to the youngster who arrived in the Island, Giancarlo Mattioli, no different from every young man setting out on an adventure, thought the world was at his feet and Jersey was just one of the places he planned to visit. 'You always want to do so much but there is a limit as to what you can do,' he said. But having tried Guernsey one winter and then being in London in 1961 - 1962, during one of the coldest winters of the time, he looked at the Island differently. 'Both Antonietta and I had a pretty rough time and we were not able to save very much. So when I got back I said this is a nice place; I am going to try and make a go of it here. Jersey is the best place to make myself a future, I said to myself, and I have been lucky because Jersey gave me that future I had looked for.'

If you have spent all your adult life based in a different country from your family, you are bound, to a greater or lesser degree, to think differently and drift apart - the influences are too great to ignore. The Italian community in Jersey shrunk in the late 1960s when Italy seemed settled into economic stability and, in some regions, major expansion. It was then that many of those working here decided to return home. On the other hand, there were those who had already been in the Island long enough to settle and to marry British girls, who had started their own families and created their own businesses. Italy was not 'home' any more. They make up the core of those who are still here and even if, according to Bruno Zunino, the Italian community has become almost small enough to be thought of as one large family. As we heard earlier, he said: 'There is no sense now, nor was there ever, of it being a community within a community with strict dividing lines, we integrated well into the local scene.'

Bruno has now been in Jersey for 60 or more years. Of course, his outlook and attitudes have changed and he maintains that the same is true for all his compatriots. As an example, he describes his sense of humour as being much more English than it is Italian. It may sound strange to others, he says, but when he returns to Italy he feels a foreigner there, much more than he does in Jersey. 'Arriva il Inglese' ('Here comes the Englishman') his relations say when he goes back to San Remo.

'But I am the lucky one. No, not just me, we all are. We were lucky to come to an Island like this and it was a good day when I got off the boat in St Helier. I think we Italians have certainly contributed to Jersey, but the Island has also been good to us.'

One of the later arrivals in Jersey, of this group at least, was Eric Ruaro. He says he goes back to Italy to his own town close to Lake Maggiore and, once there, he honestly doesn't feel completely Italian. He describes himself as feeling like a stranger in his own country even if the people he knew still treat him as if he had left yesterday. He visits his mother who lives in Pallanza (near Stresa) on Lake Maggiore, but he was born by Lake Mergozzo a few miles away.

A few years ago he went to visit the area and he found himself sitting on the wall by the lake with some companions from his youth who were telling him how the municipality was building some lovely new apartments. 'There were six being built,' Eric recalled, 'and I said it would be nice to have one but with so few being built I would never get a chance. Oh no I was told, you were born here and you go automatically to the front of the queue. I was a bit surprised but then I thought the idea of a Jersey person coming back after a lifetime away and going to the top of the housing queue (if it still happens) is not absolutely unique.'

He said he still gets an official notification from Italy every time there is a local or national election but he has never voted in Italy; he thinks it is inappropriate as he doesn't live there. 'I live in Jersey and I vote in Jersey. I can stay in Italy only for a few days before I feel I must go home - and that means here in Jersey.'

Eric could easily go back if he so wished, but Jersey is his home and Pat, his English wife, comes from Sherborne in Dorset. Jersey is where his heart is and he feels, like many of his countrymen, Jersey gave them a chance, an opportunity.

'I was the fifth from that little town to come to Jersey,' he recalled. 'Some have gone back but, looking around and thinking back, it seems that once you have stayed in Jersey for seven or eight years, that's it. You stay in Jersey. Look at me. I have the means to go and live in Italy or anywhere in Europe but there is no place like Jersey, believe you me. At the end of the day when you return by boat from France you can see the great tower blocks at Les Marais, ugly as they are, sending out a beautiful welcome message to those coming back.'

The feeling of not fitting in when revisiting Italy is very common with the Italians who settled in Jersey and Renzo Martin thinks they all have a feeling of strangeness when going back on a visit. 'In my case, perhaps I have been away too long,' he said. 'People would say the little Englishman has come to see us. I am told that now I certainly speak Italian with a bit of an English accent.'

Because of that, he does not feel he would ever be happy living in Italy again. He pointed out that living in a village has what some would see as a downside, inasmuch as everyone knows everyone in the community, so it is understood immediately why someone might take one particular point of view. However he accepts that having such a concentration of people has its good points especially when compared to a town where a feeling of isolation can swamp those living among tens of thousands of people who you can never know. Conversely, the closeness of a small community is such that you can grow away from it very quickly. 'Suddenly you don't fit in as easily as you once did, even if you try to close that gap that has grown over the years. I felt it was me having always to make the effort because I was the stranger.'

Over the years that gap had become too big for Renzo to settle down easily: 'My work has been here, in Jersey,' he said. 'My business and my contacts and my successes have all been here. The little boys with whom I used to play don't fit into that, and neither do I fit into their lives any more. Of course we are all pleased to see each other but that is not the point, we can never recover our former closeness.'

Across the age differences of this generation of Italians who came to Jersey in the 1950s through to the early 1970s, the same sense of difference, in some cases almost disenchantment, is palpable. Victor Cornaglia, for example, feels he has grown apart having been away too long. He likes going on holiday to catch up with his brother or old friends but he finds the mentality too different and staying there too long doesn't really work for him. 'In fact,' he said, 'I don't even particularly want to be buried in the family tomb.'

Paulo Crolla was head waiter for a time at Victor's restaurant, the Sea Crest. He has been in Jersey for over 40 years, coming here when he was 17 ½ from Domodossola in the Alps, just below the Simplon Pass into Switzerland. Leaving so young, his circle of friends was entirely based around school and he hasn't seen many of them since he left. 'They have all got their own lives, their own families and their own circle of friends,' he said. 'When you have been away for such a long time, it is difficult to recreate that friendship you had when you were a child. Everyone changes their outlook on life; it is all so very different and, of course, it is not just them, I have changed too, of course.'

He thinks it would be very difficult for him to live back in Italy. 'Obviously, I enjoy visiting my mother and my sister and I like to see them as much as I can. Another bonus is that I come from a beautiful, lovely mountainous region, but I couldn't live there because I am now used to Jersey life. My wife is Welsh and it would be impossible to discard all our experiences together and try to go back to my roots. Also, I think coping with the Italian bureaucracy would be very difficult; I am just not used to that way of doing things.'

But, of course, this is a purely an academic discussion for someone like Paulo, for Jersey has been a good place to be, as far as he is concerned. He has responded by working hard and - as much as he can - participating in the Jersey way of life as an Islander. 'The Island gave me a big opportunity when I came over,' he said. 'I only have good memories here. And wherever I have been or whatever I have done here, I have always been made more than welcome. No complaints whatsoever.'

Mirto Sappé has made a point of visiting his home region of Italy once a year. He still feels the pull not only of his family but also the religious connections of those Protestant valleys high up in the mountains near the French border. He has therefore kept in touch with many old friends, as well as the people he knew more as acquaintances. Until recently even his old form teacher was still around and always said hello. Mirto maintains that he was never seen as an oddity because in those valleys there was a long tradition, as with his grandfather for example, of emigrating to look for work. 'Often it was just a short journey across the border to France and then coming back to retire.

He continued: 'But nice as it is to keep in touch, I don't think, being honest, it could ever be home. Somehow, from day one I knew I would never be coming back there to live. Italy does not suit me anymore.

Perhaps it is the way things are done. It all seems just too complicated and all those endless delays get you down.'

As with the others, there is a definite pattern in attitude. The Italians in Jersey do not reject their Italian status. However, they see no conflict between acknowledging their roots while blending in to new surroundings in their adopted Island. Mirto thinks his countrymen, wherever they are, manage to preserve those two aspects of their character. Being Italian and blending in easily. Perhaps it is because they are conditioned through generations of having to go abroad to work, he thought. 'But from what I have seen and heard, whether Italians settle in Scotland or in England, in Canada, Australia or in Jersey, they take to the life as they find it there. Some of them will obviously marry some Italian women because they might have been part of the same community, who arrived together, but the vast majority of Italians marry whoever they meet and with whom they get on well. They never seem to feel that they have an obligation to marry someone from their own country.'

He accepts, in certain circumstances, the appropriateness of the previously quoted metaphor drawn from Hollywood westerns about incomers driving their covered wagons into a protective circle and firing out.

'That would be because that group, of whichever nationality, is totally committed to the traditions of old that they have left behind - no, not left behind, but brought with them,' said Mirto. 'For example I always felt that I wanted my children, who were all born here, to be brought up like everybody else. I did not want them to be different from all the people they mixed with, in school or wherever. As you might recall from your own childhood, children are very conscious of differences, and bullying - teasing at best - could be the result. Basically, I spoke English to them at home. I tried to give some background and help in other languages, in my case obviously Italian and French, but it did not work very well.'

His main aim, in bringing up his children, Mirto said, was to see them totally integrated. He says that over the past five decades or so, he knows, or has heard about, children of his friends, who insisted on speaking Italian at home, who were bullied when they went to school. He said he knows some Portuguese in Jersey who will admit that their children are picked on at school because they haven't got the language, and therefore they are different. 'Being different is a problem and results in not fitting in, whatever the cause of that difference might be. My children, as far as

I am aware, were never bullied and were always thought of, without sounding a bit pompous, as citizens of this place.'

Mauro Maori used to go back twice a year to Italy when his health allowed it. He said there was always a good family network back in Montecatini Terme and for a time he even had a flat in town so he always had somewhere to stay when he visited: 'But I certainly felt a little foreign when I was there', he said. 'When I sold Mauro's I said to Irene that we could go and live in Italy. "No," she said.

"Why not?" I asked. "You love my family."

'She replied: "Yes, but if we stay there too long you will become a proper Italian again."

He laughed as he recounted the conversation, commenting; 'I couldn't have had that, could I?'

He continued: 'Do you know, there are some who say Italy would be wonderful without the Italian civil service. Self service, rather than civil service, might be a better description. It's everywhere; even if you want to go to the loo you need a permit. And that's why I don't like my country as much as you might imagine. I remember telling you about having to bribe an official to get my papers in order to leave Italy all those years ago and nothing seems to have changed. You still have to put money down to have something that is not a privilege to be paid for, but a right. It shouldn't be the case. Yes, I suppose at the time the country had its problems and so everyone was looking after themselves. There was a huge communist presence then and there was fighting. If you want to understand how it was, read the Don Camillo stories.'

For Maurizio, Jersey offered him the chance at the right time of his life and he was able to make something of it. He looks back to his younger days with the large brigades - 50 or 60 in each - at the Grand and the Hotel L'Horizon and the characters he has met over the years. 'When I arrived, John Wileman was L'Horizon's general manager, Mrs Yvonne Simms was his assistant and Gerald Fletcher, just retired as head of Jersey Hospitality, was a trainee manager. There has been a whole generation of people, not all Italian by any means, around whom my life in Jersey has revolved, and I have been very privileged to be of that generation.'

Maurizio and his wife Sally went travelling in Europe together for a while but he eventually came back to Jersey and set up home. Was that planned?

'Living on an Island, it is very difficult to move along to the next city. I couldn't do here what I was doing in Switzerland and Germany and move around the big hotels, but despite being very happy and having a good life, we lived a lot for the moment and had no idea, nor indeed any real plans, to stay here. That all changed when the children were born. A long-term decision had to be made. This was our home and this is where we were going to stay.'

He has done his best to bring up his children, Giorgina and Marcello, as bi-lingual, not to make them little Italians, but so that they can communicate with their relations back in Italy. Maurizio recognises that travelling and working in different countries and then settling in Jersey was bound to change him and so help him develop in a very different way from the man he might otherwise have been.

'Things look a bit odd when you come back and it would be very difficult for me, let alone my family, to adjust to that way of life,' he said. 'I do feel a bit of a stranger back in Italy.

'Let me give you one example. We used to visit my parents every year. I would be chatting away and Sally would dig me in the ribs and ask why I was speaking English to my Mother. You see in Jersey, we Italians all speak Italian to each other but there are times when it is easier or simpler to use English so we all happily switch between the two languages. You take that as normal living here, but it sounds very strange out in the countryside near Rome.'

The Italian connection is being diluted in the next generation, but it is still there for his two children Giorgina and Marcello. He thinks his daughter Giorgina sees herself as a little more Italian than Marcello. 'She loves Italy more, I am sure, and goes there more often. She also enjoys Italian food and speaking Italian more than him but they both keep in touch and visit their many relatives in Italy and make sure they still have that Italian element in their lives. Marcello's son Valentino goes to Italian classes run by Serafina Venticinque so the connection goes on.'

The late Giuseppe Francescon kept in close touch with his Italian family and would often visit his village and he could see how, during his time in Jersey, his country has changed, certainly economically. 'Obviously there is much higher employment over the past decade or two and things have been looking up,' he once told me. 'However, I never took the opportunity to go back to live there, because I have always been very happy to be here.

This is where I live and in all my life I have only worked in Italy for one year - that was in Venice.'

So Jersey was Giuseppe's home. The same is true for many of his compatriots; they are local residents who came here originally from somewhere else and have done well and who happen to be Italian. As he said, he never thought of going back to live in Italy, but when he did go back to his family village, how did he feel?

'Wherever you work you always learn something new, said Giuseppe. 'It doesn't matter whether it is a pizzeria or a little pasta place or a high class restaurant, you always learn something, always. You are always changing, so the man who goes back to his village on a visit with his "foreign" family is not the same as the young boy who left.'

Giuseppe explained that his little village has only got about 750 inhabitants and so when he went back to visit he could see the shutters opening and people saying who is that? Then they would come out and say hello, it was always great to go back. He kept in touch; one of his brothers always lived there and one of his daughters got married there. But as he said, he wouldn't like to live there as, after a certain age, it is too difficult to settle down into a different way of life. 'I like Jersey,' he said. 'I think it is a beautiful Island and it should be respected for what it is and I am very happy here, so there we go.'

But going back and visiting your family can create its own difficulties as Giuseppe Ferri remembers. He used to go back to Piacenza twice a year, then his mother passed away and he carried on going, as long as his father was alive, at least once a year but, in a way, like many in that situation, he felt a bit of a stranger. In fact he expressed his feelings in more or less the same way as Paulo Crolla who had said: 'Everyone I had known was happy to see me but, after so many years away, your friends have gone, inasmuch as they have had a different life, and you have nothing left in common anymore.'

As he explained there are the relations who are always glad to see you and re-establish connections and catch up with your news but somehow, without your mother and father, it is not quite the same even with brothers and sisters. 'I think it is because they feel so obliged to welcome you and do everything they can for you but your arrival changes all their routines. Here, for example, not too long ago, some of the family came to stay in Jersey. I showed them their room, I was welcoming and friendly but after a bit, I said: "Here is a car you can use; there are the buses, please yourself. You have the freedom to do what you want."'

In Italy, he explained, it is very different. 'Frankly, I prefer to stay in a little guest house so I won't bother my relations. Then my wife and I can explore the city together and see my sister once a day and so enjoy her company. But they don't understand it, they get upset. Frankly by the time you have finished contributing to your stay, buying things, too many things, out of embarrassment, it would be cheaper to stay in a hotel.'

Visiting Italy is one thing, but Ferri wouldn't dream of going back to live there. The situation there is terrible he feels. He also thinks the government can't govern as it has run out of money. The camorra, the mafia and the other gangs are everywhere and the country is in chaos. 'I have three children working in Jersey, good qualifications, steady jobs, my life is here now.'

As he said: 'One of the reasons for coming to Jersey was to find a chance to have work and better myself, but I hoped for the opportunity of having a family who would have a better start than I ever had back in Italy. For example, my daughter went to university in Southampton, had a job with Digital Jersey and moved on. She has done very well is now the marketing manager for Jersey Post. I am very happy and she has never been a day without work. I am happy for my children and I am proud with what they have achieved and that is because of the start, my work, and Jersey, has given them.'

'To be honest, Jersey has given us more than our country has ever given us, that's for sure. The love of your country never changes - that remains constant. I am one hundred percent Italian and I will never change. As I said, I love my country even if I would never, now, live there. But Jersey gave me the opportunity to better myself and allowed me to pass on that opportunity to my children.'

Ferri's summary of his relationship with Jersey could apply to many, not least Giovanni Venticinque. He, as we have learnt, arrived in Jersey from Sicily, having served a time in the Italian Army. He left, having spent some time trying to find worthwhile work to bring up a family, so when a friend of his father, who had travelled a bit, said to him: 'Take up a small bag with what are your essentials and go. This place is not for you,' he took his advice.

It was good advice. He became a general manager of a large hotel, gained respect from all his friends and fellow Italians in Jersey and was awarded the Stella del Lavoro, later becoming a Cavaliere. 'Funny,' he said to me once. 'When I was younger I wanted to be one of those Italian émigrés who goes abroad to make a fortune and comes back very rich. I wanted to buy a huge castle and live like a lord. Dreams eh?' Dreams indeed, but he goes back to Sicily now having made a success of his life, with his eldest daughter, Serafina, being made consular agent, and with the signs of recognition for his work, as well as his community service, from the Italian government. Who needs a large draughty castle?

As he said: 'I go back now and I have done well but not to that scale I dreamt of. In one way I feel a visitor but in another I remain part of the scene. I am invited to the local town hall, given a little reception, oh yes I am certainly treated with respect.

'Could I live there now you ask? Oh no. It is something about the mentality there; it is not me anymore, it is alien. When I go back I love seeing my town and I feel great, but living there, that's different. Others have said the same thing I know and, as someone said, there are no Italian civil servants in Jersey, which makes a difference. I could certainly live with the food though.

Angelo Saccone also visits Sicily regularly, going back to see his family in Palermo but, in a sense, he also finds himself being viewed as a tourist. 'I have lost my real Sicilian accent,' he says. 'Well, you never lose it completely, but I get a strange look and they ask: "Where are you from? Are you really Italian?" I find it really funny to be treated as a foreigner in my country of origin.'

Angelo likes going back to see his family: 'But I don't like the way they go on and on about things and get involved in endless discussions and never get things done. And the way they drive!' But there is one aspect of Sicily which, as with Giovanni Venticinque, he will always hold dear: 'I love the way they eat, that is something special. But, that apart, I prefer the organised way of life here, the cleanliness, and the organisation. On the whole, things work In Jersey and, above all, without those delays, at least not those endless Italian delays.'

Franco Gatti has no one close left in Italy now. 'You ask me if I would go back to live? Oh my God no, you must be joking. I have been here 55 years. My family - that is my wife, daughter and two grandsons - are all here and, think about it, all the memories of my adult life are based here. So since you ask, I think I have done well because I achieved what I have achieved - with some help along the way for which I am always grateful - and I could give my daughter and grandchildren a better start than I had.'

It is a universal theme from the Italians in Jersey. They did well and they learnt English, which were two of the reasons for coming here in the first place. But, of equal importance, were the opportunities, much better opportunities than they feel they had themselves, which they created for their children and grandchildren. Giovanni Venticinque makes the same point: 'Looking around the successful businessmen in Jersey who happen to be Italian you see how well they have done and what a start they have given to the next generation. Bankers, senior executives, police, lawyers, civil servants, a local head teacher, a dentist - even a president of Rotary... the roll-call goes on, and that is a tribute to their parents' hard work and their successful integration.'

He continued: 'That was one of the reasons for leaving Italy. My daughter is the consular agent now, and she is arranging a cultural festival to celebrate the Italian connection and the next generation of Italians are all stepping up to help. In a way, it is difficult for us, the originals, because the new generation has a different mentality and different ideas but that is our legacy and it is our success story.'

Eric Ruaro summed up the success of his fellow countrymen who stayed on: 'I don't know if Jersey gave us a chance but it certainly gave us the opportunity to take a chance. There is no such thing as a free lunch. You had to work hard and you had to stay smart and nimble.'

Mauro Mori agreed: 'I stayed in Jersey because I loved what I was doing. I didn't set out to be a success; I wanted to be one in a sense, because I loved my work. Whatever you do in life you must love doing it to make it a success.'

Back in the introduction to this book I quoted Franco Gatti's comment: 'Do you think anyone's interested in us waiters coming to Jersey?' Of course if they had just arrived as waiters and stayed here for a short time before leaving then the answer would have been 'No'. But the Italian time of dominance in the catering scene or, to be more precise, the time when the Italians were seen as the face of catering in Jersey, may have been many years ago but, without question, the arrival of the Italians in an austerity ridden, insular, tourism industry had a huge impact.

It is worth recalling the words of Robin Seymour, the chairman of his family-owned Jersey hotel company, who has told us that they brought a much-needed professionalism to the industry, as they brought with them influences of best practice from Europe rather than just relying on a traditional British seaside offering.

To summarise much of what has been said before, the Italians, crucially, brought with them the discipline and skills of the brigade and the experience of those brigades in some of the best hotels in Europe. They arrived in Jersey keen to celebrate their own catering heritage and far-sighted hoteliers gave the maîtres and chefs their freedom to recruit the brigades within an agreed budget. At the beginning of the season, therefore, hotels would open with a trained staff who, from the most humble commis to the maître knew each other, were properly trained and who could communicate effectively with the customers. That whole package was revolutionary at the time and of immense benefit to the changing tourism industry. Who knows, if it were possible to apply, it could be equally revolutionary and beneficial now.

Another theme which comes out very strongly, as we have learnt, is one of integration. The Italian community was very open and fluid and did not shut itself in a closed room denying entry to everyone else. They arrived with learning English as one of their major aims, as competency in the language was seen as a necessary skill to have and so advance a career. Many married British girls who they met in the normal way any young man and young woman meet, and - it has been said before but bears repeating - the successful Italians have achieved the status of successful businessmen whose nationality was immaterial to their acceptance.

So in essence, the Italians had a huge influence on Jersey tourism and their legacy is immense and very important. They opened up Jersey to European catering influences, and their success was a major feature in Jersey Tourism advertising. Their own creations of such celebrations as the Italian Food Fair in Halkett Place (the forerunner of all such events) and of course the AMIRA eno-gastronomic evenings, created an industry that could develop and stay in tune with those times.

Promotional advertisements would feature members of the community showing Jersey as a destination for discerning diners so, in other words, the Italians created a starting point for development of a truly international offering for Jersey Tourism.

It could be argued, and I would not disagree, that without that contribution, the current generation of chefs and restaurateurs would not have found a fertile ground for their own ideas to flourish. Indeed we can repeat what John Wileman, the manager of the Hotel 'Horizon from 1966 until the mid-1980s said: 'The Italians of the 1960s and 1970s formed the bedrock of the fine Island cuisine of today.'

The next generation of Jersey-Italians, many half Italians, have formed a committee to create Viva Italia, a cultural festival to celebrate many aspects of their heritage. They have been bequeathed their local heritage by their parents who worked what would nowadays be seen as disgracefully long hours, for that was the way of the world at the time. However, they persevered and succeeded brilliantly, forming a major part of a dramatic change to Jersey Tourism and to the Island's catering industry.

To do this they were aware they had to learn a new language and if they achieved all this they could retire content in the knowledge of a job well done and to have achieved their main aim of giving their children what they never had themselves: the chance to make a conscious choice from many different options as to their own career advancement. Jersey, as a whole, should be very thankful for their legacy, and the next generation, those creating Viva Italia, should be extraordinarily proud of what they achieved.

So to end where we began with an answer Franco Gatti's question: 'Do you think anyone's interested in us waiters coming to Jersey?' The answer has to be: 'Yes of course, and if not, we certainly should be.'

THE AUTHOR

Hamish Marett-Crosby is a former wine merchant who, with his Italian business partner, specialised in dealing with Jersey's hotels and restaurants. Inevitably, this involved meeting and dealing with the Italian community in Jersey. For many the Italians were the public face of catering. The many business relationships developed into an open hearted welcome by the many Italians with whom he dealt - and that developed into friendship.

His company sponsored the wines for the AMIRA events and he became an honorary member of the association helping with public relations and accompanying AMIRA members on many of their trips promoting Jersey.

After his wine company was sold in the late 1980s, Hamish spent the rest of his career as a journalist and broadcaster employed by the Jersey Evening Post and BBC Radio Jersey. His 55-minute radio programme, *'The Italians in Jersey'*, was the starting point for this book.

He continues to write a regular column for *Business Brief* and occasional articles for *RURAL - Jersey Country Life* and other magazines. His documentary work on wine for BBC local radio and for the network has resulted in three national awards presented by the United Kingdom Circle of Wine Writers, the Prix de Champagne Lanson for two years in succession, 2003 and 2004. That was followed by two nominations for the Louis Roederer Regional Wine Writer of the Year in 2005 and 2006 before being awarded that honour in 2007. Following that he has also sat as a judge for The Roederer Awards.

Hamish lives in St Martin with his wife Jeannine and, for many years, a selection of Maine Coon cats that actually controlled the house. One of them, Carruthers, distinguished himself by writing occasional reviews of feline magazines and videos for the JEP.